Solar Remodeling

By the Editors of Sunset Books and Sunset Magazine

Lane Publishing Co. • Menlo Park, California

Acknowledgments

We wish to thank the following individuals, organizations, and companies for their assistance in gathering the material for this book: Donald Aitken Associates; Jim Augustyn, Berkeley Solar Group; David A. Bainbridge, solar consultant; Polly Cooper and Kenneth Haggard, San Luis Obispo Solar Group; John Kirby, Division of Energy, Missouri Department of Natural Resources; John G. Lewis, Jr., architect; Sharon McHugh, Princeton Energy Group; Len Meserve, Nature's Way Energy Systems; James Plumb, architect; Travis Price, architect; Frank R. Schiavo, lecturer, Environmental Studies Department, San Jose State University; Solar Alternatives; Solar Components Corporation; T.E.A. Foundation; Urban Solar Energy Association (Boston); Herbert A. Wade, Division of Energy, Missouri Department of Natural Resources; and Ron Wantoch, engineer.

We also gratefully acknowledge the professionals who read our manuscript and shared their knowledge and experience with us: J. Douglas Balcomb, manager, Solar Division, Los Alamos National Laboratory; Douglas Beaman, Alternative Energy Associates; Joe Matto, Sunspace Inc.; Larry Sherwood, New England Solar Energy Association; William Shurcliff, Honorary Research Associate in Physics, Harvard University; Alex Wilson, New England Solar Energy Association; and David Wright, SEAgroup.

Finally, we extend special thanks to Holly Lyman Antolini for her thoughtful critique of the manuscript.

Supervising Editor: **Helen Sweetland**

Assistant Editor: **Scott Fitzgerrell**

Special Consultant: **Fred Nelson**
Special Projects Editor,
Sunset Magazine

Photo Editor: **JoAnn Masaoka Lewis**

Design: **Lea Damiano Phelps**

Illustrations: **Mark Pechenik**

Cover: Sunspace encloses former patio, bringing it into the house—and into the solar age. New room provides both solar heat and extra living space. Additional photos and description appear on page 64. Sunspace design: Energy Options, Inc. Photographed by Steve W. Marley. Cover design by Lynne B. Morrall and Zan Fox.

Color Photography

Tom Crane: 79. **Colin Healy:** 58 left. **Jack McDowell:** 33, 40, 42, 43, 45, 52, 59 bottom, 62, 64, 77 bottom, 80. **Don Normark:** 59 top, 77 top. **Robert Perron:** 39 top, 65, 71 bottom. **David Stubbs:** 49. **Rob Super:** 41, 44, 53, 56, 57, 61, 69, 72, 73, 74. **Helen Sweetland:** 34, 39 bottom. **Tom Wyatt:** 35, 36, 37, 38, 46, 47, 48, 50, 51, 54, 55, 58 right, 60, 63, 66, 67, 68, 70, 71 top, 75, 76, 78.

Editor, Sunset Books: David E. Clark

First printing October 1982

Contents

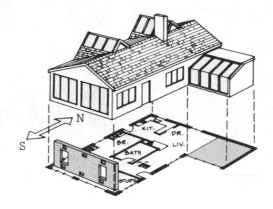

1 Solar Fundamentals

Move or improve? This is the question homeowners face when their present homes no longer suit their needs. In the past, moving was often the answer; but today more and more homeowners are choosing to rehabilitate, expand, and upgrade existing homes rather than buy new ones. Whether it comes of economic necessity or free will, it's a choice that is clear and compelling.

At the same time, rising energy costs have focused attention on the need to conserve and on the attractive notion of "going solar." So it's easy to see why more and more homeowners are looking into solar remodeling.

If you're planning an addition, there's more reason than ever to make it solar. By taking advantage of solar energy in an addition, you can add living space without increasing your monthly fuel bills; you may even be able to *decrease* your heating costs. If you don't plan to add space, there are still several simple solar remodeling strategies that you can use to reduce your consumption of conventional fuels.

Solar: Bold and new, tried and true

Solar heating—though it sounds so modern, it's hardly a new idea. City planning based on access to sunlight dates back at least to the ancient Greeks. Native Americans of the Southwest also designed their settlements to take advantage of the seasonal rhythms of the sun. Solar greenhouses go back 300 years in Europe, where botanizing aristrocrats developed them for raising plants and later took ad-

vantage of their potential for home heating. Even the solar water heater flourished in America's sunbelt at the turn of the century, before the advent of cheap oil and gas.

We're now seeing a renewal of solar thinking; people are taking up old tools and ideas, adding some new twists, and putting them to use in a new age. When the history of our era is written, it will be seen that the use of petroleum as a primary fuel was a rather brief phenomenon—on the scene, then gone, in little more than a century. And all the time, as the song says, the lucky old sun had nothing to do. Now he's going to work again.

During the winter, more energy falls on our homes than we need to heat them. In terms of astrophysics, of course, the sun is not a renewable resource; but in strictly human terms, it's a seemingly infinite one. We're now beginning to wonder how we can afford to turn our backs on such a generous source of virtually free energy. Solar design gives us the means to turn off the fossil-fuel tap, and tap instead the sun itself.

Experience in the field has shown that solar remodeling can often provide up to 40 percent of a home's heating needs. So if your home gets some sun, modern solar design can show you a way to use it. And once you put the sun to work, a measure of energy independence will be yours.

Solar for your present home

Whether you're adding a wing to the family manse, contemplating a small sunspace addition, or just looking for a way to reduce your fuel bills, there are a number of reasons why you should consider solar remodeling. Let's look at three.

Increasing energy costs. Prices of conventional fuels are sure to rise. The "energy crisis" tends to go dormant from time to time, only to emerge with renewed vigor just when we least expect it; it's easy to be alternately lulled and shocked by fuel costs.

Solar energy can give you a buffer against the shocks.

Home improvement. There are many reasons why homeowners choose to stay in their present homes rather than move. To many people, their older home is more desirable—whether because of location, size, quality of construction, or just plain charm. For others, skyrocketing mortgage rates have made moving impossible.

Whatever the reason, if you've lived in the same house for a while—or if you've just purchased a home that doesn't suit all of your family's needs—you may be thinking about expanding or upgrading it. By including solar features in the improvements you plan, you can increase the comfort of your home and—if these features are well designed and built—enhance your home's value. State and federal tax credits can often pay back part of the cost of solarizing.

Solar "intangibles." A good solar design is life-enhancing in a way that's hard to describe. There's considerable satisfaction in knowing that your home is serving at least partly as its own heater. But what may be most pleasing is that a sun-heated home is warm in a way that transcends the reading on a thermometer.

Whatever type of solar improvement you choose, you may well detect subtle changes in your living patterns—as did many of the homeowners who were interviewed for this book (and whose homes were photographed for the color gallery on pages 32–79). The owners of solarized homes often find themselves gravitating to the rooms where solar energy is at work.

The difference between a room heated by the sun's natural radiance and one warmed by the dry, artificial heat of a furnace must be experienced to be appreciated. Visit a good solar remodel and you'll see.

Passive solar versus active solar

There are two basic approaches to solar heating: *active* and *passive*. An active solar heating system is like a furnace, with the sun as its heat source. Like a furnace, it consists of mechanical components, but the hardware is different: panels of metal and glass

trap the sun's heat, a water tank or a rock bin stores it, and pipes and ducts convey it wherever it's needed. Such a system is called "active" because it depends on thermostats, fans, pumps, and valves powered by electricity to move the solar heat wherever it's needed. (For more information on active solar space heating, turn to the special feature on pages 8–9.)

In the passive approach to solar heating, a building is designed to allow the sun to warm its interior without any intermediating machinery. It stores the heat it collects within its own structure for use at night and on cloudy days, and distributes it through the interior with a minimum of mechanical aid. In short, the building serves as its own heating system.

Passive systems have several distinct advantages over active systems. Passive systems require little or no maintenance; with no machinery to break down, there are rarely any costly repairs. Most important, both their initial cost and operating costs are much lower than those of active systems, so passive systems can pay for themselves in a much shorter time. For these reasons, this book focuses on the passive approach to solar heating.

Using this book

Designed as a handbook to guide you step by step through the sometimes bewildering world of solar remodeling, this book can help you assess your home's solar potential and choose a system that can put the sun's energy to work for you. In this chapter, you'll find a discussion of the fundamental characteristics of heat, followed by an introduction to the basic passive heating and cooling systems.

Because minimizing your home's heat loss is always the first step in solar remodeling, the second chapter, "Planning Guidelines," begins with advice on insulation and weatherstripping. Guidelines for choosing the right system for your situation appear on pages 26–29, followed by a discussion of solar economics (pages 29–31) which covers payback time, loans, and tax incentives.

Throughout the first two chapters, you'll find special features that focus attention on particular topics, including active space heating systems (pages 8–9), solar-powered domestic water heaters (pages 18–19), and ways to avoid the most common pitfalls of passive solar design (page 30).

The color gallery, pages 32–79, is the real heart of the book. There you'll find a wealth of information and ideas: solar remodeling put to the test in the real world. The text and photos allow you to share the experience of people like you who rose to the challenge of bringing solar energy into their homes.

The final chapter offers 10 small-scale project ideas for the do-it-yourselfer.

You can read the book from cover to cover, or

drop into it for information on specific topics of interest; it will help you either way. The detailed table of contents will guide you to the section you need. A glossary of the sometimes arcane terms used in the world of solar design can be found on pages 93–94, followed by a list of additional resources and an index.

How Heat Moves

Heat moves naturally from warmer to cooler areas, seeking to balance the temperatures. This is a basic characteristic of heat—once you understand it, you've grasped the fundamental principle behind passive solar heating and cooling systems.

Within your house, heat flows from its source toward the chilliest nooks and crannies. If the air outside your house is cooler than the air inside, your inside heat will seek any possible route by which to continue its flow to the cold outdoors. And when it's hotter outside than in, warm air from outside will try to flow into your home's cooler interior.

Ghostlike, heat can pass right through solid walls; it can also radiate from object to object, and move with the air from room to room. These seemingly uncanny feats are performed by means of conduction, radiation, or convection.

Conduction. By passing from molecule to neighboring molecule, heat can move through a solid object, like a wall, or from one object to an adjoining one, provided the two are touching. This process is called conduction (see **Fig. 1a**). Generally, the denser the material of the wall or objects, the more quickly the heat can move. (Concrete, for example, is a better heat conductor than wood, which is less dense.)

Radiation. Like light, heat energy is radiated in electromagnetic waves (see **Fig. 1b**). This thermal radiation creates heat only when it is absorbed by an object. (This is how, on a frosty day, the sun can warm an outside wall without heating the intervening air.) Through radiation, heat appears to move in a direct line from warm objects to cooler ones, but actually, all objects radiate heat energy at all times in all directions. Warmer ones have more energy to give to this exchange, and thus cooler objects get warmer, while warmer ones get cooler.

Convection. Moving air can carry heat from warmer surfaces to cooler ones. This is called convection (see **Fig. 1c**). As air warms, it expands, becomes lighter, and rises. Then, as it passes over surrounding objects, it gives off its heat to them through conduction, cools, contracts, becomes dense, and sinks again. In a room, heat forms convective currents of rising warm air and falling cool air.

Only when air has room enough to move and establish currents, though, does convection take place. If trapped in small spaces or cavities, such as those in the weave of a sweater or in a piece of polystyrene, air becomes a good insulator, helping to prevent the transfer of heat.

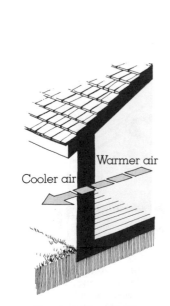

Fig. 1a Conduction

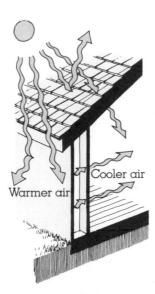

Fig. 1b Radiation

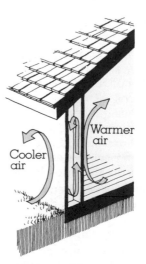

Fig. 1c Convection

For many people, the word "solar" conjures up an image of collector panels on the roof and a huge rock bin or water tank in the basement. Home heating systems that employ such components are quite different from the passive systems described in this book. Known as active systems, such heaters use thermostats, fans, and pumps (all powered by electricity) to move heat from collector panels to storage, and from storage to the house itself.

The two basic types of active systems are distinguished by the medium they use to transfer heat from collectors to storage. Liquid systems use a heat-transfer fluid such as water or a freeze-proof glycol solution; air systems, as you might guess, use air. Each type of active system also has its own type of collector, distribution system, and storage medium, but both operate on the same basic principles.

How active systems work

Active solar heating begins with solar heat collectors. These panels are usually mounted in rows on the house roof, but other locations may be chosen for better solar exposure. Like the south-facing glazing of a passively heated house, the panels in an active system should face within 30 degrees of true south (see pages 26–27) for maximum exposure to the winter sun — the closer to true south they face, the better their performance will be. They must also be tilted so that they're nearly perpendicular to the low winter sun (the exact angle of tilt is calculated according to latitude). Determining the number and size of panels necessary to heat a given house is a complex task, involving such variables as system efficiency, the size and total heat loss of the house, local climatic conditions, and the availability of sunshine.

The most common and least expensive kind of collector panel used for home space heating is called a flat plate collector. It uses a metal absorber plate to absorb sunlight, convert it to heat, and transfer the heat to the liquid or air heat-transfer medium. With liquid systems, the absorber usually consists of metal tubes either fastened to or integral with black metal plates or fins; air systems often use absorbers made of lath or corrugated metal (see **Fig. A**).

A shallow wooden or metal box, glazed on its upper surface and well insulated, houses the absorber plate. Through the greenhouse effect (see page 10), this enclosure helps trap the sun's heat in the collector.

In the morning, as soon as the collectors are 10° to 20°F warmer than the storage medium in a container in the house below (with a liquid system, this is

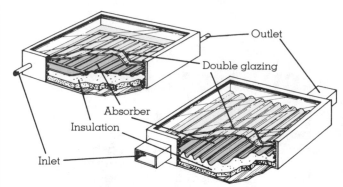

Fig. A   Flat plate collectors. Absorber in liquid-system collector (left) consists of metal tubes fastened to a metal plate; absorber in air-system collector (right) is made of corrugated metal. Both absorb sunlight, convert it to heat, and transfer it to system's heat-transfer medium.

usually a large tank; with an air system, a bin full of small rocks), a differential thermostat senses the temperature difference and turns on a pump or blower to circulate the liquid or air through the collectors.

The heat-transfer medium moves past or through the absorber, picking up heat and conveying it through insulated pipes or ducts back to the heat-storage tank or rock bin. Here, the heat is again transferred — this time out of the liquid or air and into the storage medium. Having given up its heat, the heat-transfer medium returns to the collectors for reheating. As long as the collectors are hotter than the storage medium, the heat-transfer medium will continue to circulate from collectors to storage and back again (see **Fig. B**). This

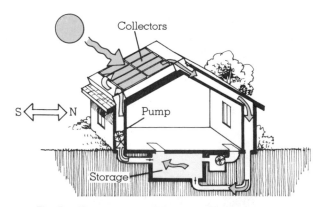

Fig. B   Heat conveyed from collectors to storage. Heat-transfer medium is pumped from storage to collectors, where it absorbs sun's radiation; medium then returns to storage, where it gives up heat.

circulation can raise storage temperatures as high as 150°F/66°C or more.

When the sun goes down (or disappears behind a cloud) and the collectors begin to cool, the thermostat shuts off the pumps or blowers as the collector temperature approaches that of the storage medium.

Meanwhile, the house has a thermostat that determines its own heating needs, just as in a conventionally heated house. When heat is needed, the thermostat turns on another set of pumps or fans that draw heat from storage to warm the house proper (see **Fig. C**).

The storage capacity of an active system usually provides from 1 to 2 days' heat for a house without any input of heat from the collectors. This protects against winter storms or cloudy periods, when a lack of direct sun prevents heat buildup in the collectors and replenishment of heat in storage.

A prolonged cloudy period will deplete the heat in storage. (Storage temperatures below about 90°F/ 32°C aren't usually high enough to be useful for space heating.) At such a time, the system becomes unable to fulfill the heating needs of the house, and an auxiliary heating system must stand in until the sun returns long enough to recharge the storage medium with heat (see **Fig. D**).

Living in an active solar home

Once you've adjusted to the visual impact of collector panels on your roof and become used to the tank or rock bin in your basement, living in an active solar

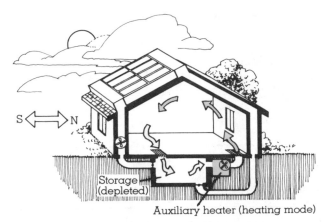

Fig. D   Auxiliary heat. When heat in storage is depleted during prolonged cloudy periods, auxiliary heater warms house.

home is much like living in a conventionally heated home. Because the heat is stored in one location, sealed off from the rest of the house, its distribution can be thermostatically controlled so that the heat is delivered only when and where it's needed, just as with a conventional heater.

Day-to-day operation of an active system, like that of a conventional heater, is relatively automatic and carefree: no manually operated vents, doors, or windows are needed for control of heat flow.

In most active systems, the auxiliary heater turns on automatically whenever stored solar heat is used up, maintaining a uniform comfort level no matter what the weather or time of day.

The question of cost

The initial cost of an active solar system is unquestionably high compared to that of a conventional heater — or of a passive solar system. In fact, on an initial cost basis alone, active solar heaters cannot usually be called economically competitive. For this reason, they're rarely installed as part of new home construction, and they're rarer still as improvements for existing homes. (Most of the collector panels now appearing on roofs around the United States actually serve systems that heat pools or supply domestic hot water — see pages 18–19.) If prices of conventional fuels continue to rise at their current rates, though, active solar may eventually become a cost-effective space heating method.

For more detailed information on active solar space heating, see the "Sunset Homeowner's Guide to Solar Heating & Cooling."

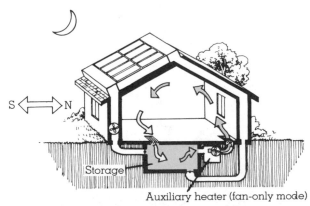

Fig. C   Heat conveyed from storage to house. Auxiliary heater — in fan-only mode — distributes warm air from storage throughout house.

A Passive Heating Primer

In order to decide which of the various passive solar heating systems is right for you, you need to understand both what they have in common and how they differ. To begin, consider the common functions that all solar heating systems must perform.

The four functions of a solar heating system

For a solar heating system to work efficiently, it must be able to perform four distinct functions: *collection* of the sun's energy, *storage* of that energy as heat, *distribution* of the heat throughout certain rooms (or the whole house), and *retention* of the heat at night and on cloudy days.

Collection. In a passive system, collection of heat is the easy part. The collection element is usually some sort of south-facing glazing (see glossary, pages 93–94) that admits the sun's radiation on sunny (or even partly overcast) days. Once this energy penetrates the glazing and strikes surfaces inside, those surfaces absorb it, become warm, and, in turn, emit long-wave radiation (which is felt as heat) that can't escape as readily through the glazing to the outside. This heat-trapping phenomenon is known as the *greenhouse effect* (see **Fig. 2**).

Why must the collection element be *south-facing*? Because, in the northern hemisphere, facing the sun means facing south.

The sun "moves" along two paths simultaneously: from east to west each day, and from north to

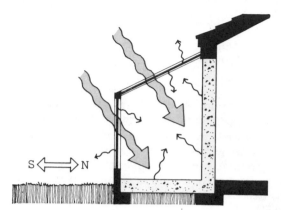

Fig. 2   Greenhouse effect. Solar radiation is converted to heat, much of which is trapped inside glazed enclosure.

south and back again over the course of each year. It rises and sets at its farthest northern point on the summer solstice—June 21. At noon on that day, the sun reaches its highest elevation of the year, appearing almost directly overhead (see **Fig. 3a**). By the winter solstice, December 21, the sun has reached its most southerly position and is at its lowest noon elevation (see **Fig. 3c**). March 21 and September 21—the vernal and autumnal equinoxes, respectively—mark the midpoints in the sun's annual treks from south to north and back again (see **Fig. 3b**).

Winter is the time when your house needs heat most, of course. As the winter sun rises in the southeast and pursues its low course across the sky to set in the southwest, the parts of your house that face south get the greatest benefit of its rays. North-facing areas, on the other hand, receive no direct sunlight at all; and rooms facing east and west get direct sun only in the morning and afternoon, respectively. So

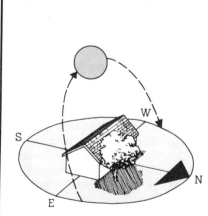

Fig. 3a   Summer solstice

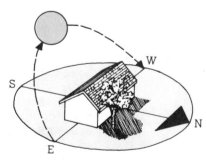

Fig. 3b   Vernal & autumnal equinoxes

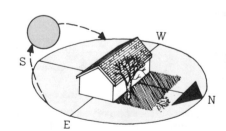

Fig. 3c   Winter solstice

the more windows you have facing south, the more heat your house will derive from the winter sun.

Storage. In passive solar designs, the heat-storage elements can be barrels, culverts, or plastic tubes filled with water, or they can be dense building materials such as brick, adobe, concrete, and stone. Forms of what solar designers call *thermal storage mass*, these elements work best when they are placed so that sunlight strikes them directly. (Wood and gypsum board also store significant heat, though they're not as efficient at it as the materials mentioned above.)

Thermal storage mass serves two purposes. It absorbs and accumulates heat during sunny days for release at night and on cloudy days; by the same token, it also helps prevent a solar space from overheating on bright days, as it takes up excess heat from the room. (Thus thermal storage mass can be helpful in summer as well as in winter; see pages 22–23.)

The amount of thermal storage mass you need depends on which type of passive system you choose; the amount of south-facing glazing in your home; your climate; the site and orientation of your house; the method you use to distribute heat (see discussion under "Direct gain," pages 11–13); how much of the thermal storage mass will be directly exposed to the sun; and the mass material. Different materials have different heat storage capacities: concrete can store 30 BTUs (see glossary) of heat per cubic foot per 1°F rise in temperature, whereas brick of average density holds 25 BTUs and water holds 62.4 BTUs. And of course storage mass with a dark-colored surface is better able to absorb sunlight.

Distribution. A strictly passive solar design relies on natural heat movement (see "How Heat Moves," page 7) to distribute BTUs throughout the portions of the house the system was designed to serve: radiation from the thermal storage mass, conduction through interior connecting walls, and convection of warm air from room to adjoining room through doorways, vents, or other openings. But many passive solar designers have found that heat distribution in passive systems is made much more effective through the use of small fans and ductwork. Because they include a mechanical (active) boost, these designs are known as *hybrid* systems. (Most of the systems featured in the color gallery of this book fall into the hybrid category.)

Retention. The same glazing surfaces that collect heat by day can lose it when the net flow of energy reverses after dark. In mild climates, double-glazed windows (two layers of glass with a ¼ to ½-inch-deep dead air space between them for insulation) may be adequate protection against nighttime heat loss. But in more severe climates, triple-glazed windows or movable insulation—curtains, shutters, or insulating panels that can be closed as sunlight

wanes—may be needed. (Movable insulation can also be useful in retarding heat gain during the summer; see pages 22–23).

The forms of movable insulation available are as various and inventive as window styles themselves, but the basic principle is usually the same. Such insulation is likely to consist of a panel or curtain made of some type of insulative material, such as fiberglass, covered polystyrene or polyurethane, layers of metalized plastic with entrapped air spaces between them, or several layers of heavy cloth. When in place, the panel or curtain fits snugly within (or over) the window frame, leaving no chinks around its edges through which air can pass.

Some types of insulating panels are attached to a window's exterior; others are mounted inside. (Because of its flammability, polystyrene is hazardous as interior insulation.) Some panels swing open like shutters; some fold aside accordion-style; some roll down like shades; and some slide away from windows on tracks, like Japanese shoji screens. Others are removed from the windows entirely during a sunny day, and put up again only when needed—at night or during a prolonged storm.

Many insulating devices are manually operated. Though they tend to be fairly simple in design and they cost nothing to operate, they require that you be on the scene, at nightfall or when a storm blows up, to put them in place. Other devices are activated automatically by thermostats. These involve some operating costs (as well as higher initial cost), but they save time and will open and close even in your absence.

Many forms of movable insulation are featured in color photographs in Chapter 3 of this book; see pages 36, 47, 48, 57, 66–67, 73, 74, and 76. In addition, several project ideas for movable insulation are offered in Chapter 4; see pages 86 and 87.

The passive solar heating "menu"

Solar designers are like chefs—they rely for their creations on a menu of time-tested entrées. Each of these entrées, or basic passive solar heating systems, has its own architectural requirements, esthetic characteristics, and operating techniques. To help you choose among them, here's a summary of the basic system types, how they function, and how they may affect your home's style and your living patterns.

Direct gain. The simplest approach to passive solar heating is known as a direct gain system. When a home is remodeled for direct solar gain, the walls or roof are "opened up" with windows that allow sunlight to penetrate directly into the living space. Rooms on the south side of the house can be ex-

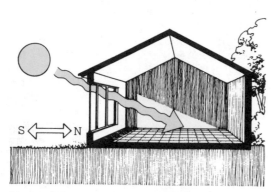

Fig. 4a   Direct gain windows (day). South-facing space is heated directly by sun; tile floor serves as thermal storage mass.

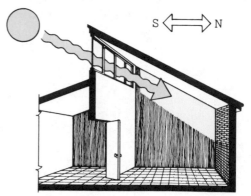

Fig. 4b   Direct gain clerestories (day). Windows project above south-facing roof and allow direct solar heating of room on north side; brick wall and tile floor serve as thermal storage mass.

posed to the sun's warming rays by means of large windows (see **Fig. 4a**) or skylights. South-facing clerestory windows can serve as passive solar "collectors" for rooms on the north side (see **Fig. 4b**).

Thermal storage mass is extremely important in direct gain systems—both to warm the living space after the sun goes down (see **Fig. 5**), and to keep it from overheating during the day. But mass also presents the biggest design problem in a direct gain system, because the heavy storage materials work best when they are incorporated into the living space where the sun can strike them directly. Some homeowners still favor the frank, high-tech look of towering water-filled columns; but there are other, more subtle approaches to the storage mass problem—including ceramic floor tiles, "thin-brick" or ceramic-tile wall coverings, and stucco plaster (applied over an existing gypsum board wall). Interior masonry walls or fireplaces can also serve as

storage mass. (For an idea on incorporating mass into your living space, see the project idea on page 91.)

With a direct gain system, distribution of heat to other parts of the house can be accomplished entirely through natural means (see page 7), or it can be assisted by a small fan. Often fan-assisted heat distribution can reduce the amount of thermal storage mass needed in a direct gain space by utilizing other mass in the house. Because the balance of heat collection, storage, and distribution is critical, particularly in larger systems, you should consult a professional when designing a direct gain system.

To retain heat at night and on cloudy days, the windows and skylights used in a direct gain system are usually double-glazed and, in cold climates, fitted with movable insulation (see **Fig. 5**). Deciduous trees, overhangs, awnings, or other shading devices can help block the sun in summer (see page 21), and interior storage mass can absorb any excess heat that builds up during the day (see pages 22–23).

The impact a direct gain system has on the appearance of a house exterior will depend largely on where the openings are located. A whole new wall of windows will obviously represent a dramatic change, but the addition of skylights or clerestory windows won't disturb your home's façade—or your privacy. The major impact of a direct gain system, of course, is on the interior of your home, where previously dusky rooms will be bathed in sunshine.

Because a direct gain system admits so much light, glare and the fading of furniture may be problems. Modern, light-diffusing glazing materials (see page 90) help spread out solar energy in the space, but because most of them are translucent rather than transparent, they'll also obscure your view. Triple glazing is another solution; it greatly reduces fading though it also reduces solar gain.

Several attractive—and efficient—direct gain

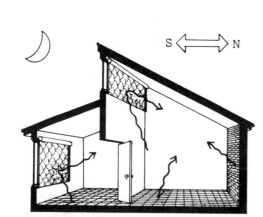

Fig. 5   Direct gain windows & clerestories (night). Brick wall and tile floor release stored heat; insulating curtains retard heat loss through glazing.

remodeling projects are featured in the color gallery on pages 34–41.

THERMAL STORAGE WALLS. Instead of allowing sunlight to penetrate directly into the living space, as in a direct gain system, a thermal storage wall puts the storage mass between the south-facing glazing and the interior of the house. The storage wall intercepts sunlight and turns it into heat, which is then delivered to the living space by means of conduction through the wall and radiation and convection in the room. Sometimes called *indirect gain* systems, thermal storage walls fall into two main categories: Trombe walls and water "walls."

Named for Dr. Felix Trombe, one of its developers, the *Trombe wall* is a south-facing thermal storage wall made of concrete, brick, stone, or adobe. It may or may not have glazed view openings in it. The entire outer face of the wall is painted a dark color or covered with selective-surface material (see glossary, pages 93–94); it's also covered on the outside by two or three layers of glazing, which are mounted several inches away from the wall and insulated around the perimeter (the glazing must be both air and watertight).

There are two types of Trombe walls: one has vents at regular intervals near the top and bottom; the other type has no vents at all.

The vented Trombe wall delivers heat in two different ways. During the day, a convection current starts when the sun heats the air between the Trombe wall and the outer glazing; as the warm air rises and flows into the house through the upper vents, cooler air near the floor of the house is pulled through the Trombe wall's lower vents into the space between the wall and the glazing, where it, in turn, is heated (see **Fig. 6a**). In addition, the heat absorbed by the Trombe wall during the day is conducted through it and, by late afternoon, begins to radiate into the house. The wall's warm inner surface also keeps warming convection currents going within the room, even after sundown (see **Fig. 6b**).

Once the sun goes down, dampers in both upper and lower vents are closed to prevent the convection current from reversing—that is, to prevent the system from drawing warm room air out through the upper vents, cooling it next to the glazing, and sending it, cold, back into the room through the lower vents. Movable insulation between the Trombe wall and the glazing helps prevent nighttime heat loss. But because such insulation is tricky to install and difficult to operate, many solar designers omit it and opt for double or triple glazing and/or a selective surface instead. (In summer, the Trombe wall is shaded and the vents are closed off tightly to prevent overheating; sometimes the wall's bottom vents are left open while vents to the outside at the top of the glazing are opened to create a cooling convection current which expels heat from the house—see page 22.)

An unvented Trombe wall doesn't provide much daytime heat, but it's useful both as a nighttime heater and, because its mass absorbs excess heat, as a means of stabilizing interior temperatures.

If your home is made of masonry, you can turn your south-facing wall into an unvented Trombe wall fairly easily and inexpensively; basically, all you have to do is have the exterior of the wall painted a dark color, and have double or triple glazing installed a few inches away from it. If you think a vented Trombe wall would suit your needs better, you may be able to have vents cut in the wall before the glazing is installed—though this will add to the expense. In either case, if your home is insulated, the insulation on the inside of the south wall will have to be removed; otherwise, heat conducted through the masonry will not be able to reach the interior.

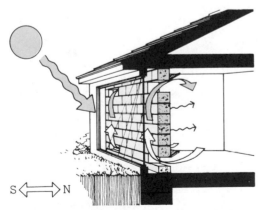

Fig. 6a Vented Trombe wall (day). Vents open, sun-heated Trombe wall warms air between wall and glazing, establishing convective heating loop.

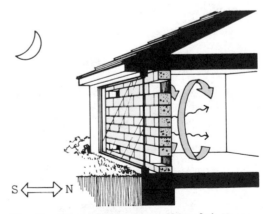

Fig. 6b Vented Trombe wall (night). Vents closed, wall's warm inner surface heats room by means of radiation and convection; selective surface coating slows heat loss from wall's outer surface through glazing.

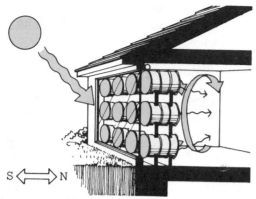

Fig. 7a "Wall" of water drums (day). Sun heats drums exposed to south-facing glazing; warm drums establish convective heating loop in room.

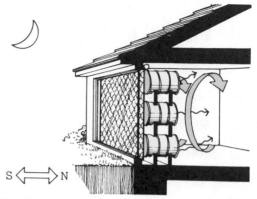

Fig. 7b "Wall" of water drums (night). Insulating curtain is lowered between drums and glazing; warm drums radiate warmth and continue convective air heating.

It's also possible to add a Trombe wall to a wood frame house, though this is a much more complicated and expensive procedure. To create a Trombe wall, a portion of the south-facing wood wall is removed and a masonry wall (usually made of concrete) and glazing are installed. The masonry wall may or may not be a load-bearing wall. Wood frame houses with recently installed Trombe walls are featured in color photographs on pages 42–43, and 46.

The interior of a room heated by an unvented Trombe wall is completely conventional in appearance; with a vented Trombe wall, the only telltale signs are the vents at regular intervals along the floor and just below the ceiling of one wall. On the exterior, however, a Trombe wall's glazing and dark surface will probably make a substantial change in the appearance of your home.

A water "wall," the other basic type of thermal storage wall, is usually not a wall at all, but rather a collection of water-filled drums, tanks, or columnlike tubes (made of plastic, fiberglass, steel ducting, or highway culvert) placed inside the house directly behind south-facing windows. These containers gather and store heat during the day and radiate it into the living space at night (see **Fig. 7a & Fig. 7b**).

Some water wall systems, especially those using columnlike tubes, are designed to allow the sun to pass between the water-filled containers directly into the living space. These combination systems take advantage of direct gain for daytime heat and indirect gain for nighttime heat (see **Fig. 8a & Fig. 8b**).

Even when containers are placed very close together (as with rows of steel drums stacked on top of one another), air can usually circulate freely between the glazing and the room. For this reason, some form of movable insulation placed between the water wall and the glazing is desirable in cold climates to prevent nighttime heat loss. (In summer, the glazing must be shaded to prevent overheating.)

The main advantage of water as a storage material is its efficiency: it picks up heat faster, holds more of it, and releases it more readily than do other types of thermal mass. But using water as a heat storage medium has several disadvantages as well.

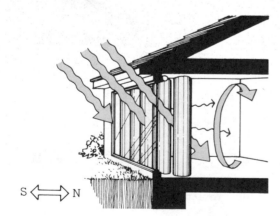

Fig. 8a "Wall" of water columns (day). Sunlight shines between columns to heat room directly, strikes columns to warm water within.

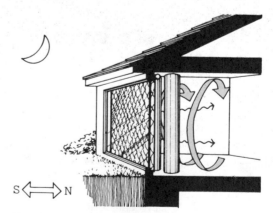

Fig. 8b "Wall" of water columns (night). With insulating curtain lowered, columns heat room by radiation and convection.

First of all, water is heavy, weighing more than 8 pounds per gallon. While concrete slab floors will generally support the extra weight, raised wooden floors might not, and reinforcement may well be necessary. Algae growth is another potential problem—though a chemical agent such as copper sulphate added to the water should keep algae in check. With metal containers, there's also a risk of leakage; to minimize the danger, containers can be lined with polyethylene, or anticorrosive stabilizers can be added to the water.

Some homeowners feel that water walls have still another disadvantage: unlike a Trombe wall, a water wall usually makes a rather bold statement in the interior scheme of a home, as well as on the exterior. But many homeowners enjoy the high-tech "sculptures" that water-filled containers represent.

Color photographs of two water wall systems are featured on pages 48 and 49 in the color gallery of this book.

Still another type of thermal storage wall is one that uses a *phase-change material* as the heat-storage medium. The phase-change materials used most commonly in passive solar design are *eutectic salts.* These salts melt (change phase) readily at fairly low temperatures (as low as 70° to 90°F/21° to 32°C) and, in so doing, store large quantities of heat, which they release as they cool and resolidify. Because phase-change materials have a very high heat-storage capacity (pound for pound, most of these salts hold many times more heat than water does), they take up much less room than other thermal storage materials, but they're usually much more expensive. Their use in passive solar designs is still experimental.

For more information on eutectic salt storage walls, turn to page 45.

Air-heating collectors. *Thermosiphoning* is another way to say "using natural convection for heat distribution"—letting heat rise naturally from its collection point into your house. A vented Trombe wall's daytime convective heating loop (see page 13) is an example of a thermosiphoning system. There are also two types of air-heating collectors that work on the thermosiphoning principle: window box heaters and thermosiphoning air panels (also known as TAPs). Unlike most direct gain and thermal storage wall systems, window box heaters and TAPs are daytime heaters only. Since these systems don't incorporate any thermal storage mass, they provide heat only when the sun is shining.

A *window box heater* is a low-cost, small-scale solar collector designed to supply up to 30 percent of the heating requirements of an average-size room. Installed in a south-facing double-hung window, it collects sunlight striking the area just below the window and delivers it indoors as heat.

The collector consists of a wooden box with a central divider, a black metal absorber, glazing,

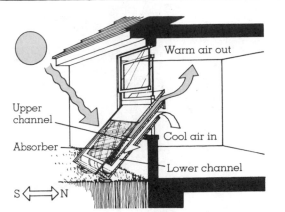

Fig. 9 Window box heater. Lath absorber converts sunlight to heat and transfers it to air (in upper channel), which then rises into house; cooler air flows into lower channel.

and some insulation (see **Fig. 9**). Air heated in the collector's upper channel rises into the house, drawing cooler house air into the lower channel and around the central divider, so that it, in turn, is heated. As long as the sun is shining, the flow continues. At night the collector fills with heavy cold air which, because it cannot rise into the room, prevents reverse thermosiphoning of warm indoor air out through the unit. (Because the collector is removable, summer overheating isn't a problem.) For additional information, see pages 84–85.

With a *thermosiphoning air panel (TAP)*, the insulated south-facing wall of a frame house actually becomes part of the solar collector. The wall's exterior siding is removed from the area of the TAP; two air vents—one near the ceiling and one near the floor of the room just inside the wall—are cut through the wall; new aluminum-foil-faced insulation is added over the exterior wall; and wood framing is installed to support a black-painted metal absorber plate and insulated glazing. An air passage behind the absorber plate opens into the house through the upper and lower vents (see **Fig. 10**).

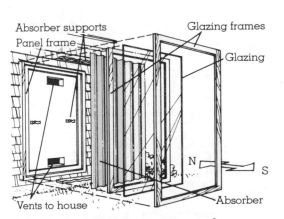

Fig. 10 Thermosiphoning air panel (exploded view)

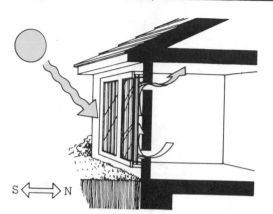

Fig. 11 Thermosiphoning air panels (operation). Sun-warmed absorber in each panel heats air behind it, establishing a convective loop.

As sunlight penetrates the glazing and strikes the metal absorber plate, the absorber gets hot and, in turn, heats the air behind it. As the air behind the absorber gets hot, it rises and enters the house through the top vent. At the same time, cooler, denser air along the floor of the interior is drawn out the bottom vent into the collector to replace the air that entered the house, thus completing the convective loop (see **Fig. 11**). Some systems use a small fan to assist natural convection. The collector delivers heat to the house as long as the sun is shining; at night and on cloudy days, a backdraft damper on the bottom vent closes automatically to prevent heat loss due to reverse thermosiphoning of warm house air to the outside. (In summer, the collectors are shaded or vented to the outdoors and the house vents are closed off tightly to keep the room from overheating.)

Because the temperature inside a TAP can exceed 200°F/93°C on a sunny winter day (and, in cold climates, drop well below freezing at night), the materials used in the collector must be able to withstand extreme temperature fluctuations.

The amount of heat that a TAP system can provide depends on the climate and the number of collector panels installed. Even an extensive multipanel system can rarely provide more than 25 percent of a home's heating needs. Still, because the initial cost of a TAP system is comparatively low, it can pay for itself in a fairly short time.

Though TAP collectors are quite obvious on the exterior of a house, they have little visual impact on the inside. Rows of vents along the top and bottom of the south-facing wall are the only interior elements.

A very efficient TAP system is featured in color photographs on pages 50–51.

Attached sunspaces. The most popular way by far to solarize an existing house is to add a sunspace (also known as a solar greenhouse, sunroom, or solarium). This section focuses on *attached* sunspaces: add-ons that are separated from the rest of the house—usually by an existing exterior wall—and that can be thermally isolated from the house, to prevent heat loss at night and on cloudy days, by closing doors, windows, and vents (see **Fig. 12**). *Integral* sunspaces, greenhouse areas that are not separated from the rest of the house, actually function as direct gain systems because they allow the sun to warm the interior of a house directly (see **Fig. 13**). Photographs of several integral sunspaces are featured in the direct gain section of the color gallery (see pages 37, 38, and 39); for information on direct gain systems, turn to pages 11–13.

An attached sunspace is basically an add-on room with a wood or metal frame, an insulated foundation, a masonry floor, and a large area of south-facing glazing. There are usually openings in the wall separating the house and the sunspace. These openings allow the warm air that builds up in the sunspace to move by natural convection into the house (see **Fig. 12**); sometimes existing windows or doors serve this function, and sometimes special vents are used. Exhaust vents in the roof or end walls of the sunspace are essential to prevent over-

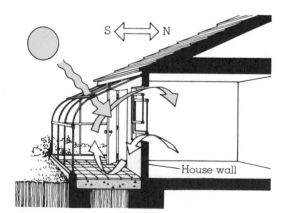

Fig. 12 Attached sunspace. Sun heats space directly; adjacent room is heated by convection through openings in house wall.

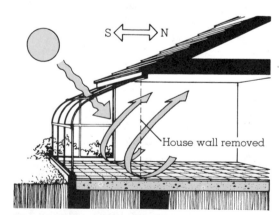

Fig. 13 Integral sunspace. Lack of dividing wall permits direct and convective heating of entire space.

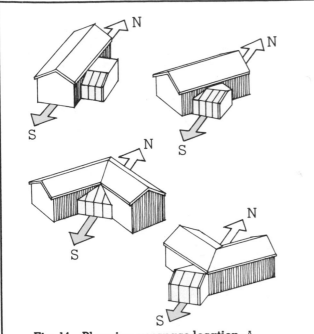

Fig. 14 Planning sunspace location. A south-facing sunspace can often be added even when house orientation is less than ideal.

heating during the summer (these vents can also be used to create a cooling convective current—see page 22). An attached sunspace is usually added along the south-facing wall of a house, but it can also be located on the east or west walls as long as the sunspace glazing can be oriented to the south (see **Fig. 14**).

Depending on how they're designed, sunspaces can provide living space, a growing area for vegetables or decorative plants, heat for the house to which they are attached, or some combination of these benefits. Because each distinct function calls for slightly different design elements, some trade-offs are necessary. If you're considering a sunspace addition, you must first decide which sunspace function is most important to you, and then have the space designed accordingly.

What are some of the variables in sunspace design? They include the slope of the south-facing glazing, the amount of glazing on the roof and on the east and west walls, and the kind and amount of thermal storage mass incorporated in the space. How you treat these variables will depend on climate and on how you plan to use your sunspace.

Sloped glazing, for example, is often used for sunspaces that are to serve as greenhouses for decorative or food plants (the slope allows greater sun penetration). But because it's less expensive to install and easier to fit with movable insulation, and doesn't present as much of an overheating problem in summer, vertical glazing is most often used if the sunspace is intended primarily as a living space.

Since a solid, insulated roof and insulated walls on the east and west will help retain heat, they too

are the rule in a solar room designed primarily for people. Plants, on the other hand, are happier if a sunspace has a glazed or partially glazed roof, and windows in its east and west walls, bathing the plants in light from several directions.

Thermal storage mass will keep both people and plants more comfortable by preventing the space from overheating during the day and by storing heat for nighttime use. But if the sunspace is intended primarily as a heater for the rest of the house (and is not to be used as a living space in the evening), thermal storage mass can actually reduce its efficiency. Most of the heat that's absorbed by thermal mass in the sunspace is unavailable to the house. If a sunspace is designed without thermal storage mass, though, a fan is often required to move warm air into the house quickly and keep the sunspace from overheating. Without some form of back-up heating, however, such a low-mass sunspace will experience large temperature variations in any climate, and can be expected to freeze occasionally in a cold climate.

In short, sunspace design is a fairly complicated matter. The best approach is to decide how you want to use the space and then consult a solar professional for a design that will suit your needs. If you're considering the purchase of a greenhouse kit (they're available from several manufacturers), it's still a good idea to consult a solar professional who can analyze both your situation and the kit design to see if it will meet your needs and expectations.

How will a sunspace affect your home's style? This will depend largely on the design and on the materials and workmanship that go into its construction. A sunspace can be a conspicuous, dramatic addition (see the homes on pages 59, 63, and 68), or it can be so well integrated into a home's design that it will look as if it had been built as part of the original construction (see pages 56–57, 60, and 61). A sunspace can be a simple, low-cost add-on or a solar show place. It depends on your needs—and your budget.

Photographs of a wide range of multifunction sunspaces are featured in the color gallery of this book; see pages 56–71.

When a sunspace is to be used *exclusively* as a heater for the house, its design is quite different from that of a multifunction sunspace. Such heat-producing sunspaces are usually tall (often two stories) and shallow, with only enough floor space to allow occasional cleaning of the inside of the glazing. The exterior house wall inside the space is sometimes painted a dark color or covered with a black metal plate to increase solar absorption.

These sunspaces typically incorporate no thermal mass, since the heat they generate goes to heat the house and not the space itself. They actually serve as huge air-heating collectors: as air is heated in the space, it rises and flows into the house through high vents, pulling cooler house air out

(Continued on page 20)

Of all the applications of solar energy, domestic water heating is by far the most cost-effective — primarily because solar water heaters operate in summer (when the most sunlight is available) as well as in winter. Most systems are designed to provide from one-half to three-fourths of a family's annual hot water needs: almost the entire supply in warm months, and lesser amounts in cold and cloudy seasons. Because they often work the year around, solar water heaters can almost always pay for themselves in less than 10 years — and sometimes in as little as 2 or 3, since tax credits apply and you can build some types yourself.

Like solar space heating systems, solar water heaters fall into two general categories: passive and active.

PASSIVE SYSTEMS

There are two basic passive systems for domestic water heating: batch water heaters and thermosiphoning water heaters. As the "passive" label implies, neither system requires pumps or automatic sensors to make it work. Both are simple, low-cost ways to introduce solar energy into your home.

BATCH WATER HEATERS. Often called "breadbox" water heaters because of the shape of their characteristic containers, batch water heaters require no energy input or specialized hardware to make them work; they just sit in the sun and get hot.

In a batch heater, the collector and storage components are one and the same — often just a glass-lined water heater tank stripped of its outer casing, insulation, and heating mechanism. The tank is painted flat black to absorb solar radiation, and is housed in an insulated box that's glazed on one side and oriented within 30 degrees of true south (see pages 26–27) in an unshaded location — usually at ground level (see **Fig. A**). Because a full tank is very heavy, roof mounting is inadvisable unless a structural engineer determines that the roof can bear the weight.

Most systems employ one or two 30 or 40-gallon tanks to preheat water on its way to a conventional heater. But in some regions, systems with two or more tanks connected in series can displace a conventional heater altogether during the sunniest months.

Freezing may be a problem in cold climates; in such areas, it's often necessary to drain down the system in winter.

Recent developments in batch heaters include the use of special glazings, reflectors, and selective-surface tank coatings to increase solar efficiency. The

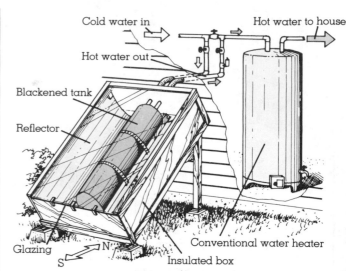

Fig. A Batch water heater. Passive solar batch heater preheats water for conventional water heater; its darkened tank serves as both collector and storage.

performance of such "enhanced" batch heaters can approach that of more sophisticated systems, and their cost-effectiveness is unrivaled. For construction hints and additional information, see pages 82–83.

THERMOSIPHONING WATER HEATERS. In all outward respects, a thermosiphoning water heater (for an explanation of thermosiphoning, see page 15) resembles a small, active liquid space heating system (see pages 8–9); the difference is that it has no pumps. Instead, the water circulates by natural convection, rising in response to the sun's heat just as air does.

To initiate this convective current, the collectors are mounted with their tops below the bottom of a well-insulated tank into which they feed (see **Fig. B**).

The storage tank is installed between the collectors and the conventional water heater, allowing water to circulate from storage to collectors and back. The solar-heated water is drawn off for household use indirectly — through the conventional heater, which acts as a backup to the solar water heater.

The system just described is called an open-loop system, because plain household water runs directly from the collectors into the storage tank. To prevent wintertime freezing, the collectors must be drained when the temperature drops.

If antifreeze is used as a heat-transfer medium (to avoid freezing problems), building codes — and com-

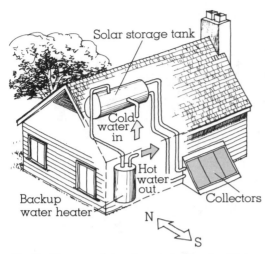

Fig. B Thermosiphoning water heater. Water warmed in solar collectors rises by natural convection to top of insulated tank set inside house above collectors; hot water is drawn off for household use through conventional heater.

mon sense — require a closed-loop system. The antifreeze circulates from the collectors to a heat exchanger — usually a long, loosely coiled copper tube or a finned device like a car radiator, double-walled for extra protection — immersed in the storage tank. This way, the antifreeze is kept separate from the water (see **Fig. C**). Heat passes from the solar-heated antifreeze to the cooler water in the tank through the walls of the heat exchanger. The coiled or finned design enhances heat exchange by providing a large area of contact between the two fluids while keeping them safely separated.

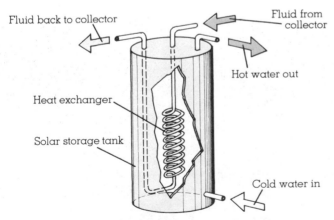

Fig. C Heat exchanger. Immersed in storage tank, coiled-tube heat exchanger provides large surface area for transfer of heat, while keeping heat-transfer fluid separate from potable water.

ACTIVE SYSTEMS

With an active solar water heater, the collectors are usually mounted on the roof, and the storage tank is placed at floor or basement level. With this arrangement, you'll need pumps, valves, and automatic controls to circulate regular household water (in an open-loop system) or antifreeze (in a closed-loop system) to the collectors and back again (see **Fig. D**).

Though some active systems are custom-built, most are available as kits for professional installation. These packaged systems include collectors, tanks, thermostats, pumps, and piping. If you have plumbing and wiring skills, you may be able to install one of these yourself on a house with a south-facing roof. Even a shed or garage roof will do: often only 1 to 2 square feet of collector area are needed per gallon of water to be heated.

These kits are less expensive than custom-built models, but they're not exactly simple to install. You'll need quite a bit of expertise and derring-do — and a good dose of patience. You'll probably have to pass a building inspection, too. Be sure before buying a kit that the instructions are adequate, or that the seller will help you if they aren't. Unless you're experienced in working with home plumbing, it's best to have your system installed by an expert, even if you have to pay more.

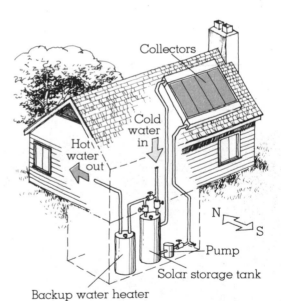

Fig. D Active solar water heater. Pump circulates heat-transfer medium from collectors to storage and back. Differential thermostat turns pump on when collectors are warmer than water in storage tank.

(Continued from page 17)

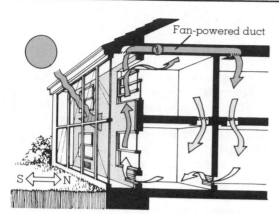

Fan-powered duct

Fig. 15 Sunspace as air-heating collector.
Narrow sunspace warms adjacent rooms by convection; fan-and-duct system moves warm air to rooms on north side.

through lower vents into the sunspace, where it, in turn, is heated (see **Fig. 15**). Fans and ducts are usually used to assist the natural convection and to circulate the heat to all parts of the house. Vents to the outdoors at the top of the sunspace exhaust hot air during the summer (they can also be used to create a cooling convective current—see page 22).

Sunspaces that serve exclusively as air-heating collectors are featured in the color gallery on pages 53–55.

Multiroom additions. When you're adding passive solar features to an existing house, the house tends to impose certain constraints on your choice of system. But if you're planning a multiroom addition, your freedom is almost as great as if you were building an entire new home. Often you can use several systems on the solar "menu" to assemble a real "gourmet dinner." Solar additions can usually be designed to supply nearly 100 percent of their own heating needs; often they can provide some heat to the rest of the house as well.

If you plan the solar features along with the rooms themselves, you can capitalize on the advantages and esthetics unique to each of the basic systems. For example, direct gain windows let in more than sunlight—they're great for views, too. This makes them a good choice for living rooms and family rooms. Trombe walls are well adapted to bedrooms, because they deliver most of their heat in the late afternoon and evening, and they could hardly offer more privacy. Sunspaces are ideal companions for kitchens, since they make cheerful breakfast nooks or dining areas. If they're also used as greenhouses, home grown lettuce can make a conveniently short trip from planting bed to salad bowl.

So if you're planning a multiroom addition, explore the creative possibilities of solar heating, and take advantage of the freedom you have. The basic systems just discussed above are precisely that:

basic. Often you can use them freely, combining and elaborating on them to create something uniquely suited to your home and your family's needs. For examples of this "gourmet" approach, see pages 72–79 in the color gallery.

The back-up: Auxiliary heating

Because solar remodeling can rarely provide 100 percent of a home's total heating needs (15 to 40 percent is much more common), your home will need to have some form of back-up system available for most of the heating season. Because your home is probably equipped with a full-size conventional furnace, you may simply want to continue using it as an auxiliary heater.

In areas where firewood is readily available, some houses can get by comfortably using high-efficiency woodstoves as back-up heat sources. Descendants of the Franklin stove, they burn wood slowly and thoroughly. Their efficient draft controls ensure that only a minimum of warm room air is drawn up the chimney. A woodstove is usually freestanding, to allow heat to radiate into the room from all its surfaces.

Woodstoves are also good sources of auxiliary heat for single or multiroom solar additions. If a woodstove isn't practical for your area (or your life style), baseboard heaters might be a good choice. These will often meet code requirements at less expense than extending or enlarging your central heating system would entail.

A Passive Cooling Primer

What makes you feel cool? The question is more complex than it seems, because the answer lies in the interaction of four variables: air temperature, air movement, temperatures of nearby surfaces, and humidity. In general, lower air temperatures, faster air movement, cooler surfaces, and lower humidity all make you feel cooler. If you can control some or all of these variables, your home will be a lot more comfortable during the cooling season. In the past, cooling strategies were likely to include liberal applications of then-cheap electrical energy. Now the sun is getting into the act.

Paradoxical as it may seem, the sun can be a great aid in cooling your house. This is easier to understand if you think of the sun as an *energy* source, not just as a *heat* source. As the cost of air conditioning rises with the cost of electricity, there's increasing interest in the sun's potential as an energy source for cooling. Though research in this field is still in its infancy, there are steps you can take today. The following discussion outlines three basic solar cooling strategies.

Reducing solar gain

Solar energy kept out of your house is solar energy you won't have to cope with as heat. Just as tightening up a house before adding a solar heating system allows the sun to work harder for you in winter, so excluding the sun in summer allows the gentle forces that power solar cooling to be more effective. Fixed and movable shades, shutters, and screens; shading from plants and trees; and adequate insulation are the keys to reducing your house's cooling needs.

Fixed and movable shades, shutters, and screens. Permanent or seasonally mounted exterior awnings, canopies, and overhangs are effective for keeping summer sunlight from striking windows. Permanent types are sized according to seasonal sun angles so that they completely shade the windows from late May to early September, but allow penetration of low-angle winter sun (see **Fig. 16**). Other options include exterior shutters and other movable shades.

If exterior shading devices aren't practical for your situation, interior shades are good (if less efficient) second choices. Perforated metal or synthetic shade screens are effective solar gain reducers, and they permit seasonal or daily operation. You can see through them, but they do greatly obscure the view—a possible disadvantage. Both roller-mounted and accordion-pleated types are available.

Though it cuts solar gain without reducing the view, reflective film applied directly to the glazing is not a good choice for shading south-facing windows. It reduces solar gain all year, so your windows can't serve as efficient "collectors" in winter.

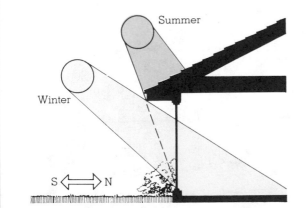

Fig. 16 Shading overhang. Overhang shades window in summer, permits direct solar gain in winter.

Ideas for several shade projects are included in Chapter 4 of this book; see pages 87, 88, and 89.

Landscaping for heat control. Nature provides deciduous trees, shrubs, and vines—all boons to the solar designer. Plant them to the southeast and southwest, where they'll shade the windows, walls, and roof during the summer. As winter approaches, your plantings will shed their leaves obligingly and present a minimal obstacle to the desirable winter sun. (Caution: The shade from large trees, even when they're bare, can reduce the performance of a passive solar system.)

Insulation. Think of insulation as a year-round investment. Remember that a tight, well-insulated house is just as important in the blaze of summer as it is in the chill of winter. Good insulation will slow daily heat build up and hold cool night air inside long into the daylight hours.

Adequate ventilation is especially important in a tight, well-insulated house; without good ventilation, the house will retain the warm air and moisture that inevitably build up during the day.

Natural and induced ventilation

Sun-blocking strategies are aimed at reducing air temperature; ventilation strategies are aimed at increasing air movement. Moving air evaporates a thin layer of perspiration on your skin—a layer whose sole purpose is to be evaporated by the breeze during warm weather, making you feel cool.

In your house, you can encourage both evaporative cooling and the replacement of warm, stale air by cooler, fresh air if you plan ventilation to take advantage of prevailing breezes. Or if summer breezes are uncommon in your climate, you can create a breeze by means of passive solar design.

Natural ventilation. In regions with dependable breezes, natural ventilation is easy to achieve. Plan for intake openings low in the windward wall, and exhaust openings as high as possible in the leeward wall. Exhaust openings should be slightly larger than intake openings. The windward openings should be well shaded by plants or shade structures to ensure the coolest intake air possible. Operable transom vents inside encourage air flow to other parts of the house.

To achieve passive humidification and cooling of the air in hot, dry climates, intakes can be located near a garden pool or dense plantings. On the other hand, passive dehumidification for hot, humid climates is still pretty much a gleam in the eye of solar researchers. The best strategy remains the one used for centuries in the American South: large-scale flow-through ventilation.

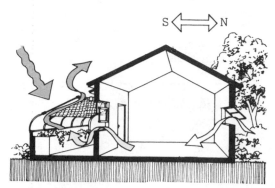

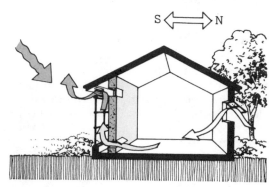

Fig. 17a   Induced ventilation (Trombe wall). Air heated between wall and glazing flows through vents to outdoors, drawing cooler air through house.

Fig. 17b   Induced ventilation (sunspace). Air is heated between overhead shade and glazing and rises through open ridge vent; cooler air is drawn through house.

Induced ventilation. As discussed on page 7, when air is heated in an enclosed space, it expands and rises. If a vent is provided at the highest point, the air will escape there and draw cooler air in through a vent positioned below. If your region doesn't have dependable winds, you can use this *thermal chimney* principle to induce your own in-house breeze.

In the cooling mode, passive systems such as vented Trombe walls (see page 13) and attached sunspaces (see pages 16–17 and 20) operate on the principle of the thermal chimney. Air warmed in these systems expands and rises to a point where, in the heating mode, it would be vented to the house. But in the cooling mode, it is vented directly to the outside from the highest possible point. Replacement air flows into the house through low, well-shaded (ideally, north-facing) vents, then streams through the house, cooling it in the process. Finally, the air enters the passive solar system, where it, in turn, is heated and vented, thus perpetuating the cycle (see **Fig. 17a & Fig. 17b**). Thermal storage mass can be helpful in such cooling schemes; once heated, the mass keeps the cooling cycle running into the evening.

Passive solar thermal chimneys, designed just for ventilation, are being used more and more. Set high in the house, the chimney's enclosed space heats up and draws a steady stream of cooler air in from windows or vents below. Thermal mass incorporated into the chimney keeps the system going after dark (see **Fig. 18**).

Radiant cooling

During the cooling season, passive solar systems incorporating mass for thermal storage can often use the mass "in reverse" as a means of lowering a home's interior surface temperatures and cooling the air. Direct gain systems (see pages 11–13), thermal storage walls (see pages 13–15), and attached

sunspaces (see pages 16–17) can all work as cooling agents if you completely shield the thermal mass from direct sun during the day and expose it to a cool clear sky at night. The night-cooled mass will absorb heat from the house by day and give it up to the sky at night. The heat energy radiates from the mass to the glazing, which then radiates it through the atmosphere into space. If all or part of the glazing can be opened at night, the mass can radiate directly to the sky, increasing cooling efficiency.

For effective radiant cooling, summer night skies have to be cool and clear. Humid night air tends to block radiation from the warm thermal mass and glazing, and hazy skies produce a greenhouse effect (see page 10) that reduces efficiency.

Movable insulation (or a shading device) that can cover glazing by day is of great importance. Usually thought of as a means of preventing heat loss during winter nights, movable insulation is equally important as a means of shading the house from the summer sun. At night, you uncover the glazing so that the thermal storage mass, charged

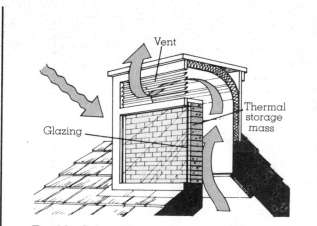

Fig. 18   Solar chimney. Air heated in chimney escapes through vent, inducing cooling air flow in house below.

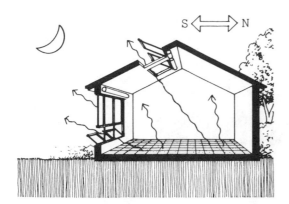

Fig. 19 **Radiant cooling.** Shaded by day, mass of house radiates stored heat to sky at night; opening the glazing enhances heat transfer.

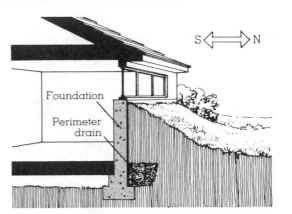

Fig. 20 **Earth berm.** Foundation extended to window sill supports sheltering earth berm; drainage and waterproofing are essential.

with your home's excess daytime heat, can radiate that heat into the night sky (see **Fig. 19**).

Earth cooling

Below the frost line, the earth temperature in a given region is very close to that region's average annual air temperature. Closer to the surface, the earth temperature varies more with the seasons, but it's still virtually immune to daily temperature swings. For this reason, earth-sheltered buildings are becoming more common. The moderating influences of stable earth temperatures offer great opportunities for stabilizing the temperature within a building.

Earth berming and earth tubes are two strategies finding increased use today. Both are best adapted to new construction, so if you're remodeling by adding on, and if you live in an area with hot summers and cold winters, earth berms and earth tubes may be worth looking into. Both must be professionally designed and tend to be expensive to install, so they're most cost-effective when they work the year around, tempering your home against both heat and cold.

Earth berms. In cold climates, berms—earth mounded against house walls and even over the roof—should be located to shield an addition from winter winds; in summer, the berms retard daytime heat buildup. In regions with hot summers and mild winters, the berms can be built on the south, east, and west, where they'll help minimize heat gain.

An addition designed for earth berming requires a professionally engineered structure—usually of masonry or concrete—wherever it will come in contact with the earth. The structure must be thoroughly waterproofed, and drainage in the berms must be carefully planned. Extending foundation walls up to windowsill height—not difficult to

do in new construction—provides for low berms at relatively low expense (see **Fig. 20**).

Earth tubes. These have always sounded good in theory: waterproof tubes, running through the earth on the cool side of the house, that would provide cool intake air as part of a ventilating and cooling scheme (see **Fig. 21**). In practice, though, problems have arisen with condensation, mustiness, and water leaks. Also, the earth surrounding the tube may heat up, rendering the tube useless.

To be effective, earth tubes need to be professionally designed for each situation, as climate and site variables greatly affect every aspect of design. In general, though, tubes are located on the north side of a building and made of fiberglass or plastic pipe, though other materials have also been used.

A recent development is the closed-loop earth tube, which starts and ends at the house. A fan circulates only the house air through the tube, improving cooling efficiency by avoiding continuous induction of hot outside air, which can cause overheating of the earth.

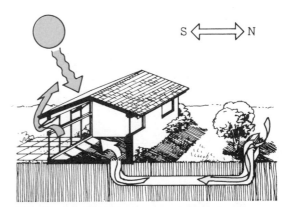

Fig. 21 **Earth tube.** Air drawn through tube from shaded location to house is cooled by the surrounding earth.

2 Planning Guidelines

Designing and building a successful passive solar heating system for an existing home isn't a simple task, but one that requires careful preparation, deliberation, calculation—and common sense. This chapter is meant to set you on the right path.

The first big step is to make sure that your home is weathertight. If you fail to weatherize before you solarize, the solar energy you collect will go right out the window (or up the chimney, or through any one of the many other escape routes that your home provides).

After you've met the sun halfway with a weathertight house that will retain heat effectively, you can go on to consider which kind of passive solar system will best suit your needs. First look at your overall regional climate—the demands it makes and the gifts it bestows on the houses in your locale. Then narrow your perspective and look closely at your microclimate—the weather patterns peculiar to the surroundings of your own home. Once you've reconnoitered the site, it's time to size up the solar potential of the house itself by considering its orientation, structure, and floor plan. Of course, your budget and your family's needs and life style will also figure in your choice of a solar system.

As soon as you've appraised your home's solar potential and selected a system, it's time to decide who will design and build it. If you're an experienced do-it-yourselfer, you may wish to handle these tasks yourself—especially if you're planning to add a small-scale system such as an air-heating collector. But if the system you want requires major structural work and you lack the necessary technical background in engineering and construction, you'll probably want to hire a solar architect, designer, or engineer to design your system and prepare working drawings, and a licensed contractor with solar experience to do the building.

Finally, there are costs to consider. Does solar remodeling make economic sense? Can you find financing? What about tax breaks?

For assistance in finding sound answers and making solid judgments, read through the guidelines in this chapter. There's no single sure path to a satisfactory solar system; but by weighing the advice given here, and adding some deliberation and homework of your own, you should end up with a system well suited to your life style and your heating and cooling needs.

The First Step: Buttoning Up

The sun is a capricious heater. Here today when the sky is blue, it may be gone tomorrow behind a layer of storm clouds. Solar radiation is both low in concentration and intermittent, often disappearing when it's most needed. As one scientist put it, the sun is "a part-time performer in a full-time world." The challenge in passive solar design is to capture, accumulate, and store enough of the sun's sporadic radiance to keep your home comfortable during the nights and stormy days, as well as during the sunny periods.

Your home itself forms the foundation of good

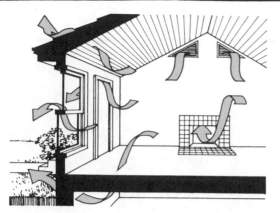

Fig. 1   Heat loss. Any surface, opening, or joint is a potential source of heat loss through conduction, radiation, and/or convection.

passive solar design. If it's drafty and uninsulated, it will never retain the sun's low-intensity heat long enough to make solar heating practical. All solar experts agree that, prosaic through it may seem, you must minimize your home's heat loss before you consider adding a solar system.

Where heat escapes

Your house has many potential trouble spots where heat can be lost during the winter or gained during the summer (see **Fig. 1**). The first culprits are your walls, roof, and floors: these, if uninsulated, can rob you of two-thirds of your heat through conduction, radiation, and convection (see page 7). You can also lose heat because of air infiltration through cracks and joints, around window and door frames, through interior walls between heated and unheated areas, and through exterior walls near the foundation.

The next culprits are your windows and doors. Though windows generally make up less of your home's total surface area than walls or roof, they lose much more heat per square foot, especially if they're single-glazed. Windows and doors together may steal as much as one-third of your heat.

Finally, you stand to lose some heat through vents and chimneys, and the openings made for plumbing and wiring; uninsulated heating ducts, water heaters, and hot-water pipes are also sources of heat loss.

Blocking the escape routes

Remember that it's decidedly cheaper to *conserve* energy than it is to *replace* it. Proper insulation, weatherstripping, caulking, and storm doors and storm windows (or double-glazed windows) constitute the simplest, most cost-effective strategy there is for conserving energy. They're also the minimum basic requirements for any home that's about to be solarized—barricades against heat loss in winter and heat gain in summer. They're described in detail, accompanied by installation instructions, in the *Sunset* book *Do-It-Yourself Insulation & Weatherstripping*.

Choosing a System

Once your house is as weathertight and well insulated as possible, you're ready to consider which solar system or combination of systems might be most suitable for your situation. (For an introduction to the basic systems, see pages 11–17 and 20–23.) To make your decision, you'll need to examine your house's climate and microclimate, then look at its siting, form, and structure; finally, you'll need to take a hard look at your budget. Each of these factors can greatly influence your choice of solar system.

Climate and microclimate

Regional climatic factors such as average air temperatures, seasonal amounts of sunshine, annual precipitation, humidity, and seasonal wind speed and direction form the background for your home's *microclimate*—the set of specific climate conditions peculiar to your home and its site. Topography, landscaping, and proximity to surrounding buildings, hills, lakes, trees, and open plains can greatly influence these background conditions, and must also be taken into consideration.

For solar heating, the most important aspect of your microclimate is the amount of direct sunlight your home's south side receives between the hours of 9 A.M. and 3 P.M. during the winter. Solar cooling relies on somewhat different factors—dependable breezes, substantial shading, and sun for induced ventilation (see page 22).

Magnetic south (as shown on a compass) and true south are rarely the same. Deviations of more than 20 degrees occur in some parts of the country. Because most passive systems work best when oriented within 30 degrees of *solar south* (that is, true south), it's important to learn what this is in your area. Fortunately, the means for doing so are as close as your local newspaper.

Using your paper's daily listing of the times of sunrise and sunset, compute the time that is exactly midway between them. This time is called *solar noon*, and may or may not coincide with noon on the clock. A plumb bob or any similar combination of a

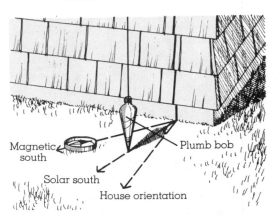

Fig. 2 Finding solar south. True (solar) south can vary considerably from magnetic south; "south" wall of house may not face either direction exactly.

string and a weight, when suspended above the ground and observed at solar noon, will cast a shadow that points true north. The exact opposite direction is solar south (see **Fig. 2**).

Your home's potential for meeting its heating and cooling requirements is best determined by direct observation during the appropriate season. It's ideal if you can keep notes for a year while you tighten up and insulate your home, letting your solar plans evolve and mature.

During each season, observe the patterns of sunlight and shadow on your home's south side. Remember that shadows are much longer in winter than in summer; winter is the time to measure their length and see if they'll affect your plans. (Shading from telephone poles and thin deciduous trees won't matter, but the long shadows cast by mountains and mountainous buildings will.)

Climate and microclimate can influence your choice of system, as well as certain aspects of its design. For example, an unvented Trombe wall, which requires steady sun, may be unsuited to a location that's periodically shaded during the day; but TAPs might work well in the same location, since they respond quickly to the sun and are self-damping when it disappears. Where sunlight is intermittent due to shading or weather, direct gain systems are more effective when fitted with motorized thermal curtains controlled by sun sensors.

The sizing of thermal storage mass in sunspaces and direct gain systems depends in part on climate and microclimate. For example, in the American Northeast and Northwest, where winter sun is often diffuse, such systems are commonly designed with little storage mass; in the Southwest, where winter sun is much more intense, the reverse is true.

You should note prevailing wind directions, so that you can shield your house in winter (with trees or other windbreaks) but use summer breezes (which usually come from a different direction) by

means of correctly placed inlets and exhaust vents.

Don't forget that your microclimate can be changed—for example, by the addition of windbreaks and shade structures. Other changes in the microclimate, such as the sudden sprouting of an extra story on a neighbor's house, are sometimes out of your hands, though in some states your right to solar access may be protected by law.

For most remodeling situations, your own observations will be enough to allow you to make a rough estimate of your home's solar heating and cooling potential. If no clear picture emerges, or if you want exact data, consult a solar professional (see page 29). Solar experts work with tables of climatic data and well-tested formulas to estimate the potential of a given site and type of system. For major remodeling projects, this is definitely the route to travel.

Looking at your house

Once you've made an inventory of your solar "natural resources," you should look at your house itself. Consider its siting and orientation, form and floor plan, and, finally, its structure.

Siting and orientation. Begin by making an inventory of your south-facing walls and roof. You may find that no part of your home faces exactly south, but remember that variations of up to 30 degrees east or west of south still offer potential for many solar designs. Once you've found solar south (see discussion at left and **Fig. 2**), you can check exact deviations from south with a compass or protractor.

Your inventory of the south-facing walls and roof will give you a picture of your home's orientation. Now you should make a sketch of the general form of your house and the rough shape of your lot. This will give you a picture of your home's siting—how and where it sits on your land. On this sketch you can also note the advantages and disadvantages you've observed in your investigation of microclimate (see above), sketching in seasonal shading and the directions of prevailing winds. Now you're ready to move indoors.

House form and floor plan. The ideal solar house is rather long and narrow, with its long axis running east and west. By now, you know how close your house comes to this ideal. The next step is to sketch the layout of rooms in your home; their placement is important in your choice of solar system.

If, in addition to an east-west form, your home has day-use spaces (kitchen, dining area, and living or family room) that are located to the south, and south walls that are unshaded in winter, congratulations—your home is truly an ideal solar subject. All options are open to you, from simple

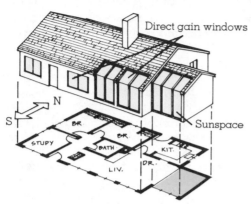

Fig. 3 Ideal orientation & floor plan. Solar remodeling is easy when day-use rooms are located to the south.

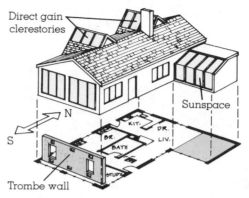

Fig. 4 Departing from the ideal. Same floor plan turned 90 degrees can still be solarized—with a bit of imagination.

window box collectors to attached sunspaces (see **Fig. 3**).

Of course, departures from the ideal are common, and many effective solar installations have been achieved under less than ideal conditions (see **Fig. 4**). For example, when day-use spaces are located to the north, you may be able to bring in sunlight through south-facing clerestories and skylights, or move warm air from a collection point on the south side by means of fans and ducts. If your house lies along a north-south axis, you can add a south-facing sunspace to an east or west wall. You might consider direct gain for an east-facing kitchen or breakfast room, since such spaces need an early morning warmup. Or install reflective insulating shutters, like those shown on page 87, to bounce solar energy into east and west windows and north-facing skylights.

The color gallery of this book features several excellent designs for awkward sun-catching situations (see especially pages 41, 66–67, and 70). All of these were professionally designed; expert help in such situations is extremely valuable.

House structure. Once you've studied the microclimate, siting and orientation, and form and room placement of your house, your final choice of a solar system may well depend on the actual structure of your house.

Residential construction is almost always of wood (either frame or post-and-beam) or masonry (brick, adobe and concrete block, and stone). Often a frame structure will be partly or entirely covered with masonry veneer, but it's still a frame house, structurally speaking. Each type of construction has its advantages and disadvantages when you want to solarize.

Wood construction, with its relatively light-weight members, is fairly easy to remodel. Often you can cut holes in exterior walls at will (building codes are quite specific about what needs to be done to ensure structural integrity). For this reason,

direct-gain windows are usually easy to add; so are TAPs. On the other hand, it's not always cost-effective to tear down a frame or post-and-beam wall and erect a masonry Trombe wall in its place. (Sometimes masonry veneers can be adapted, however.)

Unless a wooden home is erected on a concrete slab, it's often difficult to build in adequate thermal storage mass for direct gain systems. But sometimes it's possible to add a concrete slab over a reinforced wooden floor, or to reinforce an area of floor to bear the weight of water containers. Attached sunspaces, usually easy to add to wooden houses, solve the thermal storage problem easily: during construction, you can add as much mass to the sunspace as needed.

Masonry construction is much harder to remodel than wood construction. Since walls are bonded into monolithic structures, you can't cut holes in them without considerable labor—and certainly not without approval from your building department, which may require an engineering analysis. So masonry houses are not easily adapted to direct gain systems, unless the systems are designed to employ existing windows. But it's fairly easy to add an attached sunspace to a masonry house, especially where existing doors and windows can be used for heat circulation.

The chief advantage of masonry for solar remodeling lies in its mass. South-facing masonry walls can often be transformed into Trombe walls quickly and quite economically. If you insulate the exteriors of north, east, and west-facing walls, you'll incorporate valuable storage mass into a masonry home (though at the expense of the masonry's appearance on the outside). This mass can be used in both heating and cooling schemes, adding a "thermal flywheel" that helps to even out daily and seasonal temperature swings. (For more on the role of mass in solar heating and cooling, see pages 11 and 22–23.)

Budget

The preceding discussion should have given you some ideas about which solar designs might work for your home. But the "bottom line" is that the system you choose must fit your budget as well as your home and your heating needs.

Certainly the least expensive solar heating device is the window box collector (see the project idea on pages 84–85). Next in expense, probably, is the thermosiphoning air panel; this device, though easy to build, does require more expertise than a window box, because holes must be cut for it in an exterior wall. Trombe wall conversions of structural masonry walls probably come next in the scale of expense (though they're far more complex and technically demanding). Then come systems that add floor space to your house (sunspaces, for example), and those involving extensive structural modifications (clerestories on a flat roof, for example). Adding or enlarging south-facing windows for increased solar gain can be a simple task in some cases, a major remodeling project in others.

Somewhere along the line from relatively inexpensive to more costly solar remodeling projects, you'll probably reach a point where the system in question would cost more than you can manage with cash on hand, and would have to be financed like any major home improvement. A discussion of solar economics begins on this page; it includes information about financing, payback time, and solar tax credits.

Solar Professionals

If you're an experienced do-it-yourselfer, you can probably add small-scale solar systems such as air-heating collectors to your house yourself. But if the system you want will require major structural work, and if you expect it to contribute substantially to your home's heating, then you should probably get professional help. For larger projects, dollars spent on expert advice are dollars well spent: a solar professional can make the difference between satisfaction and disappointment once the project is completed.

Help comes in many forms. The solar expert you choose may be an architect, designer, contractor, or solar consultant—and sometimes all of the above rolled into one. You can hire an expert on an hourly basis to help you check out and develop your own plans, or you can turn over the entire project from conception to completion. In either case, you're look-

ing for both technical advice and design expertise that will ensure the success of your project.

Technical advice ranges from virtual guesswork, through the knowledgeable use of standard solar calculation tables, to full-blown computer simulations of every day of every conceivable year. Though there's room for most approaches, the "barnstorming" days are clearly over in the solar field. With so many qualified professionals available, there's no reason to settle for a "seat-of-the-pants" design. You can expect responsible solar professionals to use and be comfortable with tables of regional *insolation* and *degree days* (see glossary, pages 93–94) and the field-tested formulas for sizing mass, glazing, and floor area. Professionals can also advise you on possible building code restrictions and can assist you in obtaining any necessary permits and approvals.

Computers represent the state of the art in solar design today. Performance-calculation programs exist for everything from programmable hand-held calculators to large time-share computers. These programs are proving to be quite reliable in the field; new homes and remodeling projects designed with their aid perform very nearly as predicted.

Design expertise comes increasingly from the engineering and architectural community, but there are many able builders who specialize in solar work. In any case, you should not entrust your project to a designer or builder lacking in solar expertise; a background in conventional building isn't enough.

Finding the help you need. How do you find an able professional? How do you know you're buying solar sense and not solar "snake oil"? A call to your local solar energy association (see resource list, page 95), or even a quick look in the Yellow Pages under "Solar" and "Energy Management & Conservation Consultants" will yield many names, especially in urban areas. How do you sort them out?

The best method is to interview several and investigate their "track records." Ask each one for the names of several recent clients, then call those clients and chat about their experiences with the designer. If you can, visit their homes and examine both the workmanship of the solar design and the way it seems to be performing. You'll find that a clear pattern begins to emerge; you'll also gain important first-hand experience that will make you a better judge of solar design and a better-informed client.

Solar Economics

For many people, the primary appeal of a solar heating and cooling system is that it runs on vast resources of free sunlight instead of on ever-costlier oil, gas, or electricity. As you embark on a solar remodeling project, though, it soon becomes obvious that, while sunlight is free, building materials and solar expertise are not.

How do you know if the solar system you're planning will contribute enough energy to your home to make it worthwhile? Can you secure a loan that will allow you to spread the initial cost of an addition or improvement over a number of years? Will Uncle Sam pick up any of the tab? You'll need answers to these questions in order to determine if the system you're contemplating will meet your expectations—and your budget.

Payback time

Here's a question frequently asked by homeowners: How soon will my system pay for itself? When will the solar energy that my home collects actually be *free?* In order to predict your system's payback time, you must be able to estimate the amount of heat that it will provide each year. Estimates of potential system performance involve fairly complicated calculations that take into account such factors as the orientation, slope, and square footage of your solar collection area (south-facing glazing), available

FIVE PASSIVE PITFALLS

Achieving balanced, controlled passive solar heating is elegantly simple at its best, frustratingly difficult at its worst. Here are the most common pitfalls.

Failure to observe the microclimate. The first step in designing a system is to be sure that it will fit your microclimate (see pages 26–27). Passive systems are "site-specific" — they must be designed to work in harmony with local conditions. Failure to make accurate observations of the amount, direction, and duration of sunshine, wind, and shading can lead to errors in system sizing, siting, and orientation. By the same token, you should never "lift" a design created for some part of the country other than yours: don't assume that it will perform well in your region.

Inadequate shading and insulation of glazing. To reap the full benefits of an attached sunspace or direct gain system, be sure to provide movable insulation adequate to cover glazing at night in winter; otherwise, most of the heat you gain during the day may be lost to the outdoors at night. Exterior and interior insulating shutters and shades are available commercially, or you can make them yourself (see the project ideas on pages 86 and 87).

Conversely, you must also be sure to provide shading for your glazing during the day in summer, to prevent overheating. Deciduous vegetation and fixed or movable exterior shades are your best bets for this purpose.

Inadequate venting. This leads to overheating in sunspaces and direct gain systems, too. Fortunately, there are reliable tables and formulas for sizing vents; you just have to be able to use them (solar professionals can help). If you're doing your planning in the dead of winter, it may require a leap of the imagination to conjure up the idea of overheating. But don't neglect

it, or a winter's failure of the imagination may lead to many summers of unpleasant reality.

Incorrect mass-to-glazing ratio. As you may have gathered from the preceding discussion, the key to designing an efficient direct gain system or attached sunspace lies in the control and storage of solar gain. Shading and venting are two means to this end; another is determining the correct mass-to-glazing ratio. This ratio depends on the amount of floor space to be heated and on whether that space actually lies within the area of direct gain or is remote from it. With too little thermal storage mass, the space will be too cool at night — perhaps to the point where it steals heat from the rest of the house.

Again, there are formulas, tables, and computer programs for calculating the optimum ratios of glazing to mass to floor area. To use them properly, you'll find the advice of an experienced professional helpful.

Poor heat distribution. Purely passive heat circulation is a wonderful concept, but in many remodeling situations, it's an elusive reality. You can't always rely entirely on natural convection to move heated air around your home; a judicious dose of electricity, in the form of a fan and duct system, can work wonders. Fans can be especially important when a sunspace is designed to contribute significantly to heating the rest of the house (and they keep the sunspace from overheating by sending warm air into the house); but fans can also be important in ensuring the effectiveness of other solar designs.

If the performance of your system will depend on fans and ducts, be sure they're correctly sized and designed. Fans are sized according to the number of cubic feet of air they can move per minute. Duct sizes are also critical and should be calculated carefully. Once again, expert help can be valuable.

thermal storage mass, and the amount of sunshine your system will receive. These calculations are standard, and can be done for you (for a fee) by a solar architect or designer or by a heating and cooling engineer. (If you wish to make your own calculations, consult the list on pages 94–95 for sources of further information.)

Performance calculations can be very valuable if the system you're planning is designed exclusively to provide heating and cooling—like Trombe walls and air-heating collectors, for example—and not additional living space. If you keep records of your presolar heating and cooling expenses, these calculations will make it easy for you to judge the soundness of your proposed solar energy investment. You'll be able to get some idea of what percentage of current expenses can be offset by the solar system.

It's important to remember, though, that payback estimates are just that: estimates. Your actual energy savings will depend on a number of factors, including how conscientiously you perform daily and seasonal chores such as opening and closing vents and dampers, how much conventional fuel costs rise in the coming years, and the impact that your solar system has on your family's life style. Many homeowners find that their families gravitate to the solarized rooms of the house, enabling them to lower the thermostat settings in other areas. This can result in energy savings far greater than the savings predicted on paper.

What if you're adding a sunspace or a multi-room solar addition? Can you expect such an addition to pay for itself? In terms of energy savings alone, the answer is probably no. But since these spaces provide so much more than heat, you'll still be getting an excellent return on your investment. It's best to evaluate solar additions by comparing them to conventional additions. An added sunspace will usually add heat to a house, lowering utility bills where a conventional addition would have raised them. A multiroom solar addition is less likely to lower bills, but even when it adds to utility expenses, it won't raise your monthly bills as high as a non-solar addition of comparable size would.

Loans for solar improvements

Even though in most cases solar remodeling makes a lot of economic sense, many homeowners are deterred simply because they can't afford to make the initial financial investment. For these homeowners, the dream of solarizing can still be fulfilled with the help of a loan that spreads the initial cost over a period of years. There are three basic options: equity loans, home improvement loans, and personal loans. These are readily available to qualified homeowners through personal finance companies and state or federally chartered lending institutions.

Though no federally funded loans or grants for solar improvements are available as this edition goes to press, some low-interest loans may soon be obtainable through the federally sponsored Conservation and Solar Bank. To find out if you might qualify, call or write the Conservation and Renewable Energy Inquiry and Referral Service, or consult your local solar energy association (see page 95).

Tax incentives

In order to encourage energy conservation and investment in solar and other renewable energy sources, the federal government and some state and local governments have created a variety of tax incentives in the form of credits, deductions, and exemptions. These tax aids can substantially reduce your initial installation costs, so you should keep yourself up to date on the tax breaks available for solar systems in your area.

On the federal level, current laws allow an income tax *credit* (subtracted from taxes due) of 40 percent of the cost of qualifying components in a solar system (and of certain professional fees), with a maximum allowable credit of $4,000. (If your credit exceeds the tax you owe, the balance may be carried forward to other tax years through 1987).

The regulations regarding these credits change from time to time and are somewhat confusing, but here is a rule of thumb: A component does not qualify for the tax credit if it serves a structural purpose as well as a heating purpose. In other words, south-facing windows would not qualify for the credit, whereas water-filled tubes placed in front of them would; similarly, you can't claim a credit for a load-bearing Trombe wall, but you can for the glazing that covers it.

Federal laws also allow a tax credit of 15 percent (with a maximum allowable credit of $300) for certain energy conservation equipment. Eligible for this credit would be items such as wall, ceiling, and floor insulation; movable window insulation; storm doors and windows; and automatically timed thermostats.

For more information on both renewable-energy and energy-conservation credits, check with your local Internal Revenue Service office; and when you call or visit, ask for a copy of Publication 903, "Energy Credits for Individuals."

Several states offer tax breaks of their own. California, for instance, offers an additional income tax credit, above the federal limit, that can bring your savings to 55 percent of system cost. On the local level, still more incentives are provided, ranging from property tax exemptions to loan aid. In order to determine which categories of tax aid are available to you, write to your state legislator or to your congressional representative, or write or call the Conservation and Renewable Energy Inquiry and Referral Service or your local solar energy association.

3 SOLAR SUCCESS STORIES

Solar glamour, solar gifts — this sunspace addition offers both. Spa makes it a delightful living space; extensive glazing and thermal storage mass in floor make it a powerful solar heater. In summer, shade cloth covers overhead glass; deciduous vines growing on trellis will shade vertical glazing. Design: Tim Magee/Rainshadow. (For more attached sunspaces, see pages 56–71.)

DIRECT GAIN SYSTEMS

System described on pages 11–13

CONTEMPORARY COUNTERPOINT

Several solar strategies are working simultaneously in this contemporary Connecticut home. When the owners added a new master bedroom wing, they took the opportunity to bring light, heat, and a feeling of spaciousness into their living room, as well. The room's south-facing wall was moved out and opened to the sun, and three operable skylights were installed overhead. A new tile floor serves as thermal storage mass to keep the space warm well into the evening and to prevent it from overheating on bright winter days. In summer, open skylights create a cooling thermal chimney effect (see page 22).

Two heat-producing sunspaces were also added in the remodeling process: one serves as an entry vestibule and plant greenhouse; the other houses a hot tub. In winter, warm sunspace air is vented into the house; in summer, it's vented to the outdoors.

Remodeling architect: Stephen Lasar.

Small windows didn't take full advantage of this contemporary home's optimal orientation — or of its sylvan setting.

A battery of skylights and large double-glazed windows put sun to work. New master bedroom wing, far right, features large direct gain windows and roof-mounted collectors for a solar water heater.

Living room sun bath is provided courtesy of enlarged windows and newly installed skylights. Windows and vents (below skylights) draw warm air into house from sunspace below.

Split personality

Little has changed on the street side of this Virginia house since it was built just after the Civil War, but at the rear, comprehensive remodeling of the home's south side has updated it for a sunny future. Now it sports an automated direct gain solar heating system.

Each floor was extended 8 feet and enclosed with an expanse of single-pane glass. Sunlight entering through the windows heats the home directly. A fan-powered duct picks up warm air that stratifies high in the two-story solar space and sends it on to rooms on the north side. The old exterior brick walls, left exposed inside the house, store heat for nighttime release.

A sun sensor triggers motorized thermal curtains that rise when the sun is out and fall when it's not. With the flip of a switch, the sensor can work in reverse; during the cooling season, it lowers the curtains when the sun appears and raises them at night.

Solar design: Kenneth Schaal/Common Wealth Solar Services.

Two-story glass wall faces sun and view. Sun sensor operates motorized thermal curtains, raising them for direct gain in winter, lowering them to block sun in summer.

Historic façade on house's north side dates back to Civil War era; it gives no hint of the sophisticated solar features found on remodeled south side.

Thermal mass is provided by home's old exterior brick walls (area beyond them has been added). Second-floor balcony stops short of glass to allow air circulation. Reflective curtain bounces heat away in summer, keeps it in during winter.

Communing with nature in comfort

The owners of this Massachusetts home can enjoy their yard the year around — thanks to an integral sunspace that provides a panoramic view of the changing seasons, along with solar energy and light. With the old first-floor exterior wall removed, the sunspace serves as an extension of both the living room and dining room; solar energy now penetrates directly into the original portions of those rooms, as well. In addition, when the existing (now interior) second-story windows are open, warm air flows naturally into the upstairs bedrooms.

The handsome tile floor acts as thermal storage mass to warm the space after dark and keep it from overheating on bright winter days. In summer, interior shades roll down to cover the overhead glazing, and vents concealed behind doors high on the side walls exhaust hot air.

The solar design also includes a fan-and-duct system that can be used in cold weather to pull warm air from the peak of the sunspace into an underground rock bin, where the heat is stored for later distribution. In summer, the same system can draw cooler air from the rock bin into the house. The mechanical components are rarely used, though. Careful design enables the owners to rely mainly on purely passive methods of heat distribution and ventilation to keep their home comfortable.

Remodeling architects: Davies & Bibbins. Solar system design: Norman B. Saunders. Solar heating engineer: Robert O. Smith.

Almost-alfresco dining — even in winter — is one of the many benefits of this two-story-high sunspace. Sunlight penetrates directly into first-floor rooms; warm air flows into second story through existing windows. In winter, fan housed in duct at left can be used to direct heat from peak of sunspace into underground rock bin for storage; in summer, fan can draw cooler air from rock bin into house.

Carefully integrated sunspace is as pleasing on the outside as it is within. Overhead glazing continues slope of original roof. Skylights over now-interior windows admit sunlight into upstairs bedrooms.

Poinsettias in profusion grace glazed kitchen extension. Expanse of double-pane glass allows direct solar gain; energy is stored in terra cotta floor for later release.

Bringing in the sun

Solar heat, sunlight, space for plants, and a view of the woods and fields — all these were design considerations for this integral sunspace added to a remodeled Connecticut barn. Outside, the stone foundation and the sloped glazing (which matches the pitch of the entry roof) harmonize with the rest of the house. Inside, heavy terra cotta pavers unite the kitchen and its glazed extension, and serve as thermal storage mass for direct gain solar energy.

The radiant warmth of the floor and the sunspace's double glazing help to keep the kitchen comfortable on winter evenings. In summer, trees to the west and southwest shade the glazing and prevent overheating; a new entry door and operable transom window in the west wall are used for venting.

Since this is primarily a weekend house, night insulation for the sunspace glazing wasn't cost-effective; it would be, if the house were a full-time residence.

Sunspace architect: Clifford A. Cooper.

Harmonious combination of converted barn and direct gain kitchen sunspace makes a subtle solar statement.

From gloomy wing to solar show place

Privacy was the prime consideration when the service wing of this Colonial Revival house was built in 1910. Most of the vast south wall was windowless. But now, a totally revamped interior and a receptive south wall have transformed the dismal, drafty wing into a solar-heated show place.

The two-story integral sunspace and large double-glazed windows on both floors of the wing invite the sun indoors. The new tile floor serves as thermal mass, helping to prevent overheating on bright winter days and storing heat for nighttime release. The wing can be heated by the home's conventional furnace, but even in the cold climate of Connecticut, an efficient, centrally located woodstove is the only back-up that's needed. A shading system to prevent summer overheating is now in the planning stages.

In addition to the changes on the south wall, the original kitchen was completely renovated, and part of the floor between the first and second stories of the wing was removed to create a two-story-high living area. Skirting this space is a balcony reached by means of a spiral staircase at the west end of the wing; the balcony provides access to a second-floor office and guest bedroom on the north side. The open plan assists the natural distribution of warm air — as does a small fan.

Architect: Wayne Garrick/Clifford A. Cooper Architects.

Parade of parasols softens sunlight admitted through overhead glazing in integral sunspace. Tile floor stores heat for nighttime use. In addition to dining area, transformed wing includes family room and remodeled kitchen downstairs, and office and guest bedroom off balcony above.

Service wing afforded privacy, but little more.

Opened up to the sun, south wall ushers in light and heat.

Double-duty skylight system

This ingenious installation provides passive and active solar heat in winter, as well as thermal-chimney ventilation (see page 22) during warm California summers.

Four domed skylights in the roof admit sunlight to the home for direct gain heating. Tile over a concrete floor and brick over concrete-filled stud walls in the stairwell act as thermal storage mass. Mini-blinds and diffusing panels below the skylights modulate the gain.

The space between the skylight domes and diffusing panels acts as an air collector, and the blinds double as solar absorbers. The drawing shows how air rising in the space is heated, then sent to north rooms in winter or vented to the outside in summer. When warm air flows out through the turbine vent in the roof, cooler air is drawn through the house.

Solar design: Richard M. Cushing/Arc Sun Design Associates.

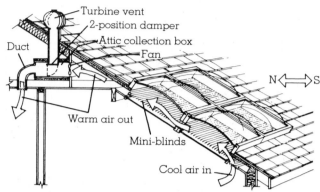

Skylight system combines both direct gain and air-handling features. Air entering system at lower end is heated as it flows past heat-absorbing blinds; warm air then enters attic distribution duct. In winter, fan moves warm air to north rooms; in summer, hot air is directed to turbine vent.

Domed skylights fill roof over family room. Turbine vent is visible above, with active solar water heating panels at right.

Skylights, tile, and brick team up for a direct gain system. Domed skylights admit sun; tile and brick provide thermal storage, gradually releasing heat as room cools after dark.

CLERESTORIES HEAT NEW NORTH ROOM

When the owners of this house in the Southwest asked for a new family room and solar heat, the architects responded with a design that's as carefully planned as it is beautiful. Floor-plan and siting constraints dictated that the new room be added on the north side, so sunlight enters through south-facing clerestory windows that project above the home's flat roof. A fan-and-duct system taps the space and sends warm air to east-facing rooms in winter; in summer, vents in the small end walls of the clerestory exhaust hot air.

The windows are recessed into a shading overhang that, together with an overhanging ledge in the room, eliminates direct sunlight in summer, but admits it in winter (see drawing). The interior overhang keeps winter sun off the furniture, yet allows it to strike a structural adobe wall at the back of the room. Insulated on the outside, this wall serves as thermal storage mass, moderating temperature swings in the room. The roof line extends beyond the wall to form a covered patio on the north for cool outdoor living in summer.

Remodeling architects: John Petronis and Toby Pugh/Architectural Research Consultants. Solar consultant: Dr. Jerry Alcone.

Overhang beneath clerestories keeps winter sun off furniture, permits it to strike adobe wall.

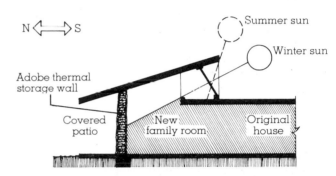

Exterior and interior overhangs control solar gain, keeping sun on mass wall.

Clerestory windows pop up above roof to scoop in sun. Overhang shields them in summer. Effective direct gain design heats north-side family room and contributes warm air to rooms on east side of house.

System described on pages 13–15

Trombe wall pays solar dividends

The owners of this northern California home say that since they replaced their south-facing frame wall with a vented Trombe wall (made of grouted concrete blocks), their conventional furnace rarely turns on in winter.

During the day, the wall heats the house primarily by a convective loop generated as air is warmed between the wall and the glazing. (A concrete pool deck on the south side of the house reflects additional sunlight onto the surface of the wall, increasing solar gain.) In the evening, vents are closed and the wall heats the house by radiation, and by convection along its inner surface.

Panels can be laid on a support structure above the new wall to shade it during the summer.

Solar design: Alfred S. Braun.

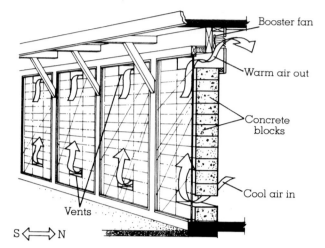

Concrete blocks replaced original frame wall. Warm air circulates by natural convection; fan boosts circulation when needed. Vents must be closed when wall cools to prevent reverse air flow from cooling the room.

Vents top and bottom allow convective air flow; their operable louvered registers have little visual impact on room.

Trombe wall is home's primary heat source in winter (note upper and lower vents). Shading panels are placed on overhead structure in summer.

Trombe wall with view

There's a dark blue Trombe wall just visible through the glazing of this Rocky Mountain home. Part of a wedge-shaped addition to the home's south side, the vented wall heats an open living-dining area above and a bedroom below. (The wedge shape corrects the home's slightly westward orientation back to true south.) In addition to providing convective heating by day, the wall gives up its stored heat to the house after dark. At night and on cloudy days, a sensor triggers motorized thermal curtains which are automatically lowered between the wall and the outer glazing to retard heat loss. In summer, the function of the curtains can be reversed; they can be lowered by day to prevent sunlight from striking the wall.

Windows added within the Trombe wall preserve views and allow for some direct gain heating. The Trombe wall works in harmony with other direct gain windows and a back-up woodstove, shown in the lower photo. Dark tile on the floor and a brick wall behind the stove add thermal storage mass.

Remodeling architect: Peter Dobrovolny/Sunup Ltd., Architects.

Dark blue Trombe wall, behind glazing at right, heats upper-floor living area and lower-floor bedroom. Windows in the wall preserve views and allow direct solar gain.

View of living room shows vents in Trombe wall, and direct gain windows. Clerestory window above adds light and more direct gain heat. Brick wall serves as thermal storage for woodstove.

Second-story sleight of hand

There's something magical about eutectic salts. A phase-change material (see page 15), they absorb vast amounts of heat per pound when they melt. As they cool, they change phase back to a solid, releasing this heat. Pound for pound, they're many times more efficient than water for storing heat.

A masonry or water thermal storage wall would have been expensive and too heavy for this second-floor bedroom addition, so a clever and inconspicuous phase-change system was designed. Behind two of the four lower panes of the bedroom windows, polyethylene rods filled with eutectic salts were installed in the stud space (see drawing). Vents top and bottom permit convective heating of the room as the rods heat up during the day. As they cool after sundown, they warm the inner wall of the room and allow further convective heating. When the heat in the rods is gone, the vents are closed to prevent reverse circulation — and cooling — of the air.

Remodeling design: Richard M. Cushing/Arc Sun Design.

Second-floor addition reaches up for solar gain. Panes at far left and right conceal pockets containing thermal storage rods. Photo shows how shading overhang reduces gain in spring, when less heat is needed.

Vents top and bottom are the only signs of the sophisticated thermal storage system detailed in drawing, below left.

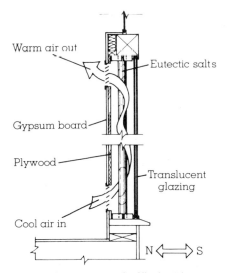

Warm air out — Eutectic salts

Gypsum board

Plywood — Translucent glazing

Cool air in

N ⟷ S

Thermal storage rods filled with eutectic salts gather heat by day, while vents permit convective air heating. After sundown, the cooling salts release radiant heat and keep the warm air flowing into the evening.

Trombe wall keeps sleeping quarters cozy

The renovation of this 150-year-old New Hampshire duplex involved much more than a face lift. The addition of an unvented Trombe wall for the bedroom wing and energy-conscious improvements throughout the house (including thorough insulation and caulking) have made the utility bills look just as attractive as the completely refurbished structure.

The unvented Trombe wall was a good choice for the bedroom wing, since it delivers most of its heat in the evening. To install the wall, an interior post-and-beam system was built to support the roof, and the existing south-facing frame wall was removed. Because thermal expansion and contraction in the severe New Hampshire winters can cause the 54-ton concrete wall to bend back and forth as much as 3 inches at the top, a system of sliding air seals, insulation, and "floating" glazing mounts was developed to allow for this movement, yet retard heat loss and prevent leaks.

Though the wall has no vents for convective heating, 4-inch-diameter plugs at the top and bottom of the wall can be removed for convective cooling in summer. Cool basement air flows into the space be-tween the wall and glazing; as it picks up heat, it rises into the attic, where it's vented to the outdoors.

Sensors placed inside selected walls of the house during renovation monitor the performance of the energy-saving improvements. Analysis of the data shows gratifying results: in the first year after renovation, the bedroom wing alone saved nearly 5,000 kilowatt-hours of electricity (roughly equivalent to 160 gallons of heating oil).

Architect: Charles E. Roy. Solar system design: T.E.A. Foundation, Inc. and Daniel J. Desmond.

150-year-old duplex needed an energy update as well as cosmetic improvements. House was practically uninsulated, and front (south side) didn't take advantage of sun.

Unvented Trombe wall keeps bedrooms warm throughout evening; windows in wall (visible through glazing) allow light to enter bedrooms during the day.

Good neighbor

This house is a special case in the world of solar remodeling: it was remodeled before it was built. Part of an experiment sponsored by a large utility company, it was redesigned to test the ease with which a commercially built house can be adapted to solar heating without drastically altering its appearance. The prospective owners were as adventurous as the utility company, so the plans for a conventional house (like the one at left in the lower photo) were revised to include a large Trombe wall and a sunspace that would also serve as an entry vestibule.

The two-story Trombe wall is the primary solar heater and thermal buffer for the house; it adjoins the living room downstairs and a bedroom upstairs. The unvented design of the wall is intended to allow it to provide most of its heat in the evening.

In summer, a roof overhang and a first-floor fixed shade keep sun away from the Trombe wall, and four pairs of buttonlike exterior vents exhaust air heated between the wall and glazing. As warm air is vented, cool air from the basement is drawn into the space between the wall and glazing, where it, in turn, is heated and vented, establishing a cooling convective current.

Architects: Don Prowler and Doug Kelbaugh for Pennsylvania Power and Light Co.

Change in wall thickness marks location of Trombe wall in a second-floor bedroom. At right, a small window with a thermal shade looks out through the Trombe wall glazing.

At home with its neighbor, solarized house at right features a two-story Trombe wall and sunspace entry vestibule, yet remains essentially conventional in appearance.

Hard-working water "wall"

Both active (see pages 8–9) and passive solar systems contribute heat to this home in northern Massachusetts. The passive system, which consists of six water-filled fiberglass columns behind double-wall fiberglass glazing, allows both direct and indirect gain.

During the day, some of the solar energy admitted by the glazing penetrates directly into the family room through the columns and the spaces between them. The rest of the energy is stored in the water for release later. When the sun disappears, a motorized thermal curtain between the columns and glazing is lowered to prevent heat loss, and the water-stored warmth is released, keeping the family room comfortable well into the evening.

A shallow addition on the home's south side provides a strategic, out-of-the-way location for the water-filled columns; the addition's concrete foundation easily bears the water's weight.

Solar system architect: Keith B. Gross.

Water "wall" allows both direct and indirect gain. Sun shines between and through columns during daylight hours. At night, motorized insulating curtain is lowered to retard heat loss through glazing, and heat stored in columns is released.

Shallow addition on home's south side houses six water-filled columns; weight of water presents no problem for addition's concrete floor. Roof of addition provides perch for active solar collectors.

Thermal counter for a cozy kitchen

A bank of steel water drums within a counter acts as "thermal ballast" to keep this kitchen sailing smoothly through the heating season; the handsome tile countertop conceals the solar secret. The hidden drums provide steady, gentle convective air heating on sunny winter days.

As the drawing and photos show, the strategy is simple. Sunlight penetrates the counter's exterior glazing and warms the ends of the drums, setting up convective currents in the water to distribute the heat throughout each drum. Air (admitted to the under-counter storage area through kick-space vents) passes among the drums, picking up the stored warmth, and rises into the room through vents near the back of the counter. Light and view are maintained by a bank of double-glazed casement windows set above the counter. These can be opened for ventilation.

The counter (see page 91 for a similar project) is part of a comprehensive solar remodeling design that includes a direct gain spa room, active solar water heating, and a stair tower that doubles as a thermal chimney (see page 22).

Remodeling architects: David Wright and Dennis A. Andrejko/SEAgroup.

Sleek tile top covers a bank of steel water drums hidden under counter. Cool air is admitted through vents in kick-space; operable louvered vents in top exhaust rising warm air. Dark tile countertop stores additional solar heat.

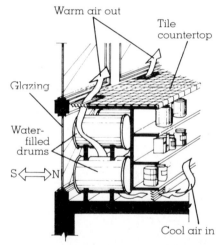

Sun strikes ends of drums through glazing, warms water within. Air moves past the drums, picks up heat, carries it to kitchen.

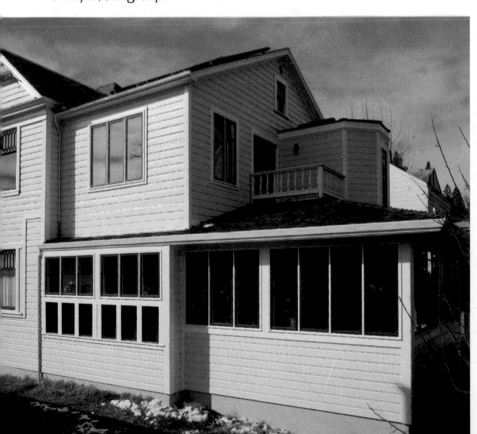

Water drums lie behind the six lower panes in kitchen addition (center). New spa room and stair tower are at right.

Systems described on pages 15–16, 17, 20

"TAP"ping the sun

Though the owners of this Massachusetts home originally planned to solarize with a sunspace, a careful microclimate analysis left them with some doubts. The south side of the house was actually 30 degrees west of solar south, and hemlock trees in a neighboring yard threatened to shade a large portion of the proposed sunspace addition by early afternoon.

Since solar heat, rather than living space or a plant-growing area, was their primary goal, the owners decided instead on a system of seven thermosiphoning air panels (TAPs). The five center panels are totally passive; the panels on either end have fans to assist the natural convection of warm air. (The fans were installed because obstructions in those areas of the wall necessitated smaller vents than originally planned.)

The air-heating collectors cost only about a fifth of what the proposed sunspace would have cost. And, despite the less-than-ideal orientation, their performance has been remarkable. In the first winter after installation, the solar system — together with several new storm windows and some additional insulation — saved nearly 250 gallons of heating oil, cutting the owners' fuel bills by almost one-third.

Solar design: William Doubleday.

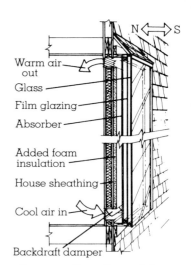

N ⟷ S

Warm air out
Glass
Film glazing
Absorber
Added foam insulation
House sheathing
Cool air in
Backdraft damper

Cross section of panel shows convective heating loop.

TAPs queue up along home's southwest wall. Panels at either end are fan assisted; five in center are purely passive. Perched above TAPs are collectors for an active solar water heating system.

Rows of vents along top and bottom of wall are TAP system's only interior elements.

A HOUSE-SIZE HEATER

When the owners of this Seattle home decided to add two new floors, they took the opportunity to add the integral two-story air-heating collector shown here.

The collector consists of a narrow space between tall windows and the home's insulated south wall. Air passing into the space from the first-floor dining room is heated well above 100°F/38°C by the time it rises to the top of the space. Sliding windows between the collector and the second and third-floor sitting rooms preserve the view and allow access to the glazing for cleaning.

In the collector, a fan-and-duct system picks up the heated air and delivers it either to the house or to a basement rock bin, where the heat is stored for later use. A coal stove provides the principal back-up heat; a duct high above the stove picks up warm air for distribution by the air-handling system.

Remodeling architects: The Hastings Group. Solar consultant: Arnie Wilson.

In third-floor sitting room, sliding windows open to solar collector, allowing view and access to glazing. Intake grille at upper left directs some warm air to conventional furnace, which can also provide back-up heat.

South-wall glazing on second and third floors encloses an air-heating collector big enough to heat entire house.

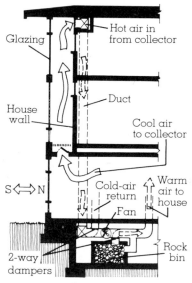

Shallow, two-story space serves as air-heating collector. Warm air is drawn from high in the space and delivered to the house — or to a basement rock bin, where its warmth can be stored for later use.

Minimum space, maximum performance

Built on the narrow south side of a Colorado house made of concrete blocks, this tall, shallow sunspace employs a unique two-stage design. Its upper chamber acts as an air-heating collector; its lower chamber is a preheater, and will eventually serve as a plant greenhouse, as well.

A fan moves hot air from the upper chamber into a duct that passes through the insulated partition between chambers and continues through the floor into the living areas set below grade. Cool air returns to the lower chamber through another duct (see drawing).

Penetrating the partition between chambers are two "stratification traps"; when the fan is on, these "traps" allow air preheated in the lower chamber to flow into the upper one, where it gets much hotter. When the sun disappears, the low-mass upper chamber cools off more quickly than the lower one, which has a high-mass floor; the "traps" then ensure that warm air in the lower chamber stays in the lower chamber — to buffer adjoining bedrooms against the cold.

Inside the lower chamber, collectors for a thermosiphoning water heater gain efficiency from the extra insulation provided by the warm space.

Design: Tom O'Brien/Solar Design.

Lower chamber contains heat duct (right) and solar water heater (center). One of the "stratification traps" is visible in ceiling at far end.

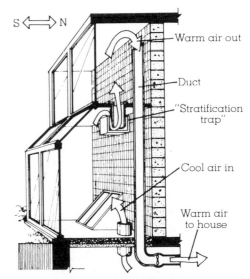

As air is drawn into house from upper chamber, preheated air from lower chamber flows through "trap" that prevents reverse flow.

Two-stage design of sunspace shows clearly in exterior view. Lower chamber preheats air; upper chamber "superheats."

A sunspace exclusively for heating & cooling

With few windows on its south wall, this contemporary Connecticut home wasn't making the most of its excellent solar orientation. But with the addition of a shallow sunspace, solar energy is helping to heat — and cool — the house.

The one-and-a-half-story sunspace is a mere 4 feet deep. The siding of the house wall within the space was stained a darker color to increase solar absorption, and sliding glass windows were installed in the house wall on each floor.

The sunspace serves as an air-heating collector in winter. Air heated in the space rises and flows through the upper windows into the kitchen and dining room; from there, natural convection distributes it to the rest of the house. Cooler air returns to the sunspace through windows in the ground-floor master bedroom. As long as the sun is shining, the convective heating cycle continues.

In summer, the sunspace becomes a thermal chimney. Air heated in the space rises and escapes through two operable skylights in the roof, drawing in cooler replacement air through open windows on all sides of the house.

A living room addition, built at the same time as the sunspace, benefits from both direct and indirect gain in winter. Sunlight is admitted to the south end of the room through large direct gain windows, and to the north end through four new clerestories positioned next to the original two. A narrow interior window and a through-wall fan bring warm air from the sunspace into the living room.

Solar design: Colin Healy and Joe Matto/ Sunspace Inc.

Living room addition profits from both direct and indirect gain. In winter, large windows admit sunlight; small interior window admits warm air from sunspace. Through-wall fan above window assists when needed.

Practically windowless, south wall of contemporary home passed up solar energy.

Shallow sunspace serves as air-heating collector in winter, thermal chimney in summer. Four panels of acrylic glazing (center of photo) admit solar energy to sunspace; operable skylights act as vents in summer. Four new clerestory windows — together with original two — deliver sunlight to north side of house. Direct gain living room addition is at right.

System described on pages 16–17, 20

High-desert harmony

Though it looks like part of the original construction, the attached sunspace was added later to this New Mexico home. The key to its successful integration: careful design meticulously executed with good materials.

Designed primarily as a living space, the sunspace was built over an existing patio and makes use of the home's original shading overhang. Materials used include laminated mahogany beams, double-pane glass, and curved double-wall acrylic glazing. The overhang was insulated during construction, and a brick-on-sand

thermal storage floor was laid on the original patio.

During the day, the space contributes substantial heat to the house through several sliding glass doors. At night, thermal shades cover the overhead glazing and combine with the insulated overhang to keep the sunspace comfortable well into the evening. The thermal shades also help prevent unwanted heat gain on hot days.

To ensure adequate ventilation in summer, casement windows were used for much of the glazing. These can be opened to the desert breezes at night, then closed against the heat of the day.

Sunspace design: Valerie Walsh/Solar Horizon.

Finely crafted sunspace lodges comfortably under existing roof overhang. Curved eave complements rounded forms of adobe house.

Retractable insulating shades ride in grooves routed in arched, laminated mahogany beams. Brick-on-sand floor provides thermal storage.

Small-scale sunspace makes big contribution

Designed primarily as a year-round greenhouse for vegetables and decorative plants, this sunspace also provides a generous amount of wintertime heat for the snug Connecticut house to which it's attached. In the first winter after the sunspace was added, the owners' fuel bills were nearly 20 percent lower than in the previous year. (Energy conservation measures in the house itself — including additional insulation and an automatic setback thermostat — have reduced those bills by another 10 percent.)

Solar energy is admitted to the sunspace through double-wall acrylic glazing. Warm air generated in the space flows into the first floor of the house through existing windows and doors; a vent at the peak of the sunspace directs warm air to an upstairs bedroom.

Sunspace planting beds receive direct sunlight during the day; at night, they're warmed by heat stored in water-filled 55-gallon drums located beneath the beds. To keep the sunspace temperature above freezing on the coldest winter nights, windows in the house wall are opened slightly to allow warm house air to flow into the space.

In summer, two domed skylights in the insulated roof and a double-hung window in the west wall of the sunspace are opened for ventilation.

Sunspace design: Colin Healy and Joe Matto/ Sunspace Inc.

Gable-end sunspace admits solar energy through double-wall acrylic glazing. Two domed skylights are used for venting in summer.

Indoor garden benefits from direct sunlight during the day; at night, it's warmed by heat stored in water-filled drums under planting beds. Warm air flows into house through vent at top of sunspace and through existing windows and doors.

Sunspace makes the most of windowless south wall

Built on a north-south axis, with no windows in its south wall, this home near Seattle was once oblivious to the sun. It has since mended its ways — thanks to a large new sunspace.

Designed for plants and indoor-outdoor living, the sunspace also supplies a good part of the home's heating needs. An expanse of overhead glazing gathers solar energy, even from overcast winter skies, and is shaded in summer to prevent overheating. An exposed-aggregate concrete floor and large, brown-painted water-filled tubes provide thermal storage. Ranked next to the tubes and handily disguised, large ducts collect heated air for fan-powered heat distribution.

With so much glazing, automatic fan-forced venting is essential in summer and during those winter days when the sun breaks through with unexpected power and the owners are away.

Sunspace design: Rob Lerner/Northern Sun.

Sunspace covers south wall of house, making the most of wall's excellent orientation. Rolls of greenhouse cloth perched above are unrolled for summer shade.

Overhead glazing coaxes heat even from cloudy skies. Water tubes and heating ducts ranked against the house wall make a bold statement. Ventilating fan is just visible high on the far wall.

A masterpiece of mimicry

Meticulous design and painstaking workmanship resulted in a sunspace so well integrated that it's virtually impossible to tell from the outside where the original house ends and the addition begins.

On sunny winter days, the sunspace not only heats itself but helps to heat the rest of the house as well. Overhead glazing and small-paned casement windows admit sunlight; warm air flows through a door at the rear of the sunspace into rooms on the home's east side. A fan-and-duct system can be used to assist the natural distribution of heat, when desired.

At night, the sunspace requires no heat from the home's conventional furnace; the warmth stored in the concrete floor — and an efficient wood-burning stove — keep the space comfortable, even on the coldest Massachusetts nights.

Sunspace architect: Gerry Ives/Lamb & Ives.

Sunspace exterior echoes design of original home down to the last detail — from shingles to small-paned windows. Front of home faces west (gables are visible above addition's overhead glazing); south-facing sunspace is tucked behind garage.

Small-paned casement windows admit more than woodland vista: they're efficient solar "collectors" in winter and can be opened for ventilation in summer. Overhead loft supports batch water heater.

Classic cottage, solar sense

Small turn-of-the-century houses like this one dot the countryside from coast to coast. When time has been kind to them, it seems a shame to alter them greatly; yet many need enlarging, updating, and rehabilitating before they can meet today's needs.

Help for this Rocky Mountain house came in the form of a new foyer on the first floor and a sunspace on the second. Throughout, the remodeling design remains faithful to the spirit and form of the original.

The sunspace, located off the master bedroom, warms quickly in the morning, thanks to a new east window. As the sun moves to the south, solar gain comes through a glazed door (which also provides access to the new deck), a new south-facing window, and an operable roof window that also vents hot air in summer. In winter, air heated in the low-mass space is ducted to north-side rooms downstairs.

Architect: Milburn/Sparn Energy Architects.

Vent in peak of sunspace channels warm air downstairs; roof window opens for summer breezes. Original gable is visible through door to new deck.

"Charming bungalow; needs work" — so the ads might have read for this classic cottage.

New sunspace above and foyer below blend seamlessly with original house. Large window faces east for morning warmup; roof window admits southern sun. New flared gable end echoes the original.

Old garage became solar office when glass replaced garage door. Bricklike tile floor serves as thermal storage mass; fan-and-duct-system moves warm air to rest of house.

FAST RELIEF

In what may be the fastest remodel in the West, this garage was solarized by the mere replacement of the garage door with a wall of windows and glass doors. The result: a home office that heats itself and generates a little extra to help heat the house.

An integral part of the small split-level house, the south-facing garage was a wintertime liability. Its leaky door was a thin barrier against winter's chill, and the integral design practically ensured a trapped pocket of cold air into which the house continuously lost heat. Now, thanks to the new glass wall, there's a pocket of warm air that remains well into the evening, and the house gains more heat than it loses.

Dark tile laid on the garage slab absorbs much of the solar energy entering through the glass wall, storing it for evening use. The concrete driveway acts as a reflector, bouncing additional sunlight into the new room. Excess warm air can be ducted to the house as needed. A shading trellis and mini-blinds provide summer shade and control of solar gain, and the glass doors at each side can be opened for ventilation.

Solar design: David R. Roberts/Dr. Solar.

A simple solution to both space and energy problems, glazed garage takes advantage of home's favorable southern orientation. At one stroke, owner got space and energy boost. Shading trellis will support deciduous vine.

Overhead "steps" regulate solar gain

Increasing their year-round living space was the owners' primary goal when they added a sunroom to their charming brick home in Massachusetts. Careful attention to detail in both design and construction resulted in a space that's comfortable in every season.

In winter, the sun is the room's primary heat source, with a woodstove for back-up. Solar energy is admitted through double-glazed windows and sliding doors, and through overhead acrylic glazing. The overhead glazing features a "Solar Staircase," a patented system of stepped reflectors that admit low-angle winter sun but exclude high-angle summer sun, helping to prevent overheating. When the room's sliding doors are opened in summer, the sunroom is transformed into an indoor-outdoor living area.

Sunspace architect: David R. Johnson. Solar system design: Norman B. Saunders.

Cantilevered over twin concrete piers, elevated sunspace is glazed overhead and on three sides. In summer, sliding glass doors open to admit cooling breezes.

"Solar Staircase" admits low-angle winter sun through overhead glazing but excludes high-angle summer sun. Woodstove in corner furnishes auxiliary heat when needed. Tile-on-concrete floor provides thermal storage mass.

Opportunity knocks

Partly damaged in a fire, this California home needed repair, so the owners decided it was time for remodeling and solarizing. The old concrete patio presented an excellent opportunity: its location was perfect for a sunspace addition — one that could be built with minimum fuss, since the house already enclosed the south-facing patio on three sides. All that was needed was to add a glazed roof and wall.

The sunspace is well integrated into the overall form of the remodeled house (see front cover photo). Its roof is a natural extension of the roof of the new second floor, and its south-facing glazed wall is aligned with the renovated house walls. Heated air from the sunspace flows into the house through doors opening onto a new balcony. There's also a duct that takes air from the sunspace peak and delivers it to a collection area (called a plenum) in the attic; from there the air is blown to north-facing rooms on the first floor. Air flows back to the sunspace through lower-floor doors. This air-handling system greatly moderates temperature swings in both the house and the sunspace.

Several design features allow easier control of heat in summer than is usual with such extensive overhead glazing. To prevent overheating, shade cloth is unrolled overhead, and vents in the sunspace soffit are opened. From these vents, air flows up along the glass to the attic plenum, then out through turbine vents. In summer, the house wall to the west blocks afternoon sun, which would otherwise be a prime source of overheating.

Remodeling design: Energy Options, Inc.

Patio enclosed on three sides provided an excellent opportunity for solar remodeling. Sunspace addition required only one glazed wall, and a glazed roof designed to meet the roofline of a new second floor.

Brick chimney once stood outside; now it provides thermal storage mass in a new sunspace. Warm air moves to the house through upper-floor ducts and doors. Air then flows down the staircase visible in background and through lower-floor doors in the sunspace.

Saltbox sprouts
a garden sunspace

This Connectict saltbox boasts a heat-producing sunspace where the garden used to be. But the solar-heated space still offers plenty of room for gardening, and is usable the year around. Beds next to the double-wall acrylic glazing and along the home's black-painted foundation nurture both decorative and food-producing plants. The plants don't freeze, even on the coldest winter nights, thanks to the insulated roof and end walls, and to heat stored in the house foundation, the water-filled drums next to the planting beds, and the earth below the beds.

On sunny days during the heating season, the sunspace also supplies a substantial amount of heat to the rest of the house. Warm air flows through a ridge vent into the first floor of the house; cooler air returns through basement doors at either end of the sun-space. In summer, hot air is vented through two skylights in the roof and an awning window in the west wall.

Sunspace design: Colin Healy and Joe Matto/ Sunspace Inc.

Planting bed along home's foundation is retained by water-filled drums (under bench), which also serve as thermal storage mass; another bed lies adjacent to sloped glazing.

On crisp autumn days like this one, sunspace helps keep saltbox cozy. Sloped double-wall acrylic glazing captures sun's energy throughout heating season. Awning window in end wall and skylights in insulated roof can be opened for summer ventilation.

Solar in the City

It would be hard to imagine a more inflexible solar remodeling situation: an old brick row house in a designated historic area of Philadelphia where no alterations could be made to the south-facing façade. There was nowhere to go but up.

A rooftop sunspace, set back beyond the parapet and invisible from the street, is the key feature in a multifaceted solar strategy that brings the old building into the modern age. Essentially a glazed box, the sunspace extends down through the roof to the third floor. The area above the original roofline is designed to overheat; a powered duct picks up hot air near the top of the space and blows it to the rest of the house. On the third-floor level, the space becomes a greenhouse where plants are bathed in indirect light. In summer, the sunspace is vented outdoors, producing a thermal chimney effect which helps to ventilate the house.

The sunspace is controlled by Beadwall insulation, a system in which polystyrene beads are blown between double panes of glass at night and on hot summer days. The blower reverses, sucking the beads back into their storage tanks, to allow solar gain in winter and natural lighting in all seasons (the south and north-facing sides are controlled separately). Existing south-facing windows boost heat through direct gain. Air circulation was enhanced by opening up the interior.

Architect: Stephan J. White. Beadwall insulation: Zomeworks Corporation.

Night falls, and so do beads. Vacuum motors blow polystyrene beads between panes of glass, buttoning up the sunspace for the night. Tanks store the beads by day. Steel duct moves warm air to the house.

Open interior, created by removing a floor, promotes air circulation. Marks in wall show where joists were removed.

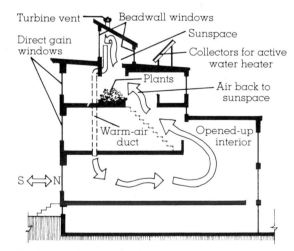

Sectional view shows how sunspace and direct gain windows work together.

Rooftop sunspace, invisible from the street, is the heart of a new solar system for this restored row house.

Unconventional wisdom

Though the shape of this New Jersey sunspace seems reversed (its high wall faces south, its low wall north), computer modeling ensured that it would work.

Shingles cover walls of grouted concrete blocks, heavily insulated on the outside. This mass and the concrete floor absorb much of the solar energy streaming in through the extensive south glazing and store it against the chill of night. In its first winter, the space fell below freezing only once — and only by one degree. The home's utility bills, though, have decreased substantially since the space was added.

Side walls and an overhang shade the upper glazing in summer. Awning windows in the knee wall, operable west-facing windows, and a continuous vent in the roof peak handle venting chores.

Sunspace design: John L. Buzzi, Jr./Sun Source, Inc. and John Lederer, AIA.

Built out from home's west wall, new sunspace faces south for sun. Side walls and overhang shade upper glazing from spring until autumn.

High south wall of sunspace admits sunlight; concrete walls and floor act as thermal storage mass, stabilizing temperature swings in all seasons. Warm air flows from sunspace into house through French doors. Continuous vent in peak ensures good ventilation in hot weather.

Plants, parties & ping-pong

The owners of this New Mexico house bought it with solar remodeling in mind. Its original patio, notched into the home's southeastern corner, is now the site of two sunspaces: a large one for family living and a smaller one for plants.

The large space supplies the house with heat by day; after nightfall, the tile-covered patio slab remains warm enough for entertaining and recreation. A glass wall facing east contributes to fast warmup after cool desert nights, and the house wall to the west blocks afternoon sun in summer.

The plant sunspace, located just west of the larger sunspace along the home's south wall, is shaded by active hot water collectors. Planting paraphernalia is handy for the owners, yet out of sight of guests.

Sunspace design: Doug Edgar/Pogo Construction.

Side-by-side sunspaces serve different purposes: one at right is for people, smaller one at left is for plants.

Built on old patio, sunspace supplies fan-forced warm air to house through registers at left and right. Four large awning windows above swing out for ventilation.

Dark tile floor absorbs heat. Sliding door at right leads to plant sunspace; another one, in glass wall at left, serves as an air intake for venting.

69

Basic geometry

How do you remodel for solar when the south-facing portion of your home is nothing more than a tree-shaded corner? Consider a triangular sunspace like the one that solved the orientation problem of this L-shaped Connecticut home. With the trees removed, the cleverly designed addition provides solar heat as well as a handsome living area.

In winter, two rows of double-glazed casement windows, overhead glazing, and an operable skylight near the peak of the sunspace serve as passive solar "collectors." As the sunspace heats up, warm air flows into the first floor of the house through iron-and-glass doors at either end of the addition, and into the upstairs master bedroom through a door off the second-floor balcony (a hot tub is recessed into the balcony floor). The sunspace floor, tile over concrete, serves as thermal storage mass to keep the addition comfortable into the evening.

When the skylight and casement windows are opened in summer, the sunspace becomes a breezy patio for indoor-outdoor living.

Sunspace design: Colin Healy and Joe Matto/ Sunspace Inc.

Only a corner of home faced solar south — and even that was partially shaded.

Cypress-lined space receives sunlight through casement windows, overhead glazing, and skylight near peak. Hexagonal tiles on floor store heat for release after sun goes down.

Triangular addition solved orientation problem; removal of trees made way for sun. Collectors for active hot water system are mounted on house roof at left.

Sunspace turns remodeled barn around

Though the old New Jersey barn was oriented along an east-west axis — ideal for solar — its siting could hardly have been worse. The barn presented two floors to the north, but only one to the south.

At the heart of the design that solved the problem is a hard-working upper-floor sunspace that serves several functions besides helping to grow plants. As the lower photo shows, the sunspace admits plenty of solar energy, which is stored in a uniquely sited "wall" of water tubes: it's outside the sunspace in a lower-floor light well. Day-use rooms are concentrated on the floor above, just across the light well from the sunspace, where they receive solar heat.

Sliding glass doors separate the sunspace from the light well. Open, the doors allow convective air heating; closed, they help prevent nighttime heat loss to the cooler sunspace. Heat stored in sunspace water drums protects the plants on freezing nights.

Architect: Harrison Fraker.

Attached sunspace is key solar feature of completely remodeled barn. Open sunspace vent, just below house eave, aids passive cooling. Direct gain windows are at left, with active solar water heating panels on roof.

Light streaming through sunspace strikes water tubes set below grade in lower-floor light well. Sunspace and light well play active role in passive heating and cooling design.

Described on page 20

Baubles, bangles & Beadwall

A lavish sunspace lies at the heart of this New Mexico solar addition which also includes a new bedroom and library. As hard-working as it is beautiful, the sunspace supplies heat to much of the house.

The vaulted acrylic roof and the glass and acrylic bay use Beadwall insulation: polystyrene beads are blown between double panes to retard nighttime heat loss in winter and to block the sun on hot summer days. To let the sun in, the blower draws the beads back into their storage tanks. The drawing shows how the zoned Beadwall system controls lighting and solar heating. The ridge can be opened for ventilation.

The new bedroom is heated by a vented adobe Trombe wall. With the onset of spring, louvered panels are added to shade the wall in stages. An unvented Trombe wall heats the library.

Addition designs: David Harrison/Sundomain Building Corp. (sunspace and bedroom); Mark Feldman and Richard Braun (library).

Added wing includes sunspace (left), master bedroom (center), and library (behind trees and in photo above). Two louvered panels shade bedroom Trombe wall.

Adobe Trombe wall heats library, part of an earlier addition.

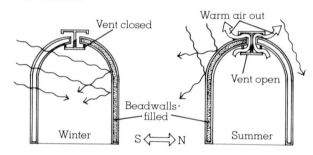

Beadwall system is zoned to allow separate control of north and south-facing halves of vault; solar energy is admitted in winter (left), and bounced away in summer (right). Ridge opens for ventilation.

Cascading beads fill vault and semicirular bay to lock in or exclude solar energy as season and time of day require. Beads in west-facing bay and north and south-facing halves of vault are separately controlled. Adobe walls and slate floor act as thermal storage mass; powered duct (out of photo) high in sunspace moves warm air to rest of house.

Ski-country chalet with quick solar reflexes

When this Rocky Mountain vacation home became a full-time residence, more room was needed. In adding on to the home's south face, the architect reoriented it for better solar exposure. The new rooms have an east-of-south bias that promotes morning warmup and minimizes the shading effect of a mountain to the southwest, which blocks the sun early on winter afternoons.

Downstairs, the addition includes a living room and a room for a new hot tub; upstairs, two bedrooms and a deck were added. Solar heating is achieved by means of large direct gain windows. A tile-covered concrete floor downstairs and three water "walls," two of them upstairs, serve as thermal storage mass.

Automatically controlled, reflective thermal curtains react quickly to the comings and goings of the often fickle mountain sun (motors raise and lower the curtains in response to a sun sensor). The function of the curtains can be reversed in summer, when they can serve as daytime shades.

Addition architect: Peter Dobrovolny/Sunup Ltd., Architects.

Curtains up, the sun floods in. Water "wall" is concealed at center; only its vents give it away.

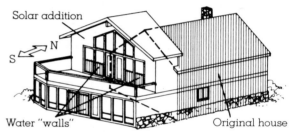

Solar addition faces east of south, away from a shading mountain and toward sun and view.

When sun hides and snow flurries begin, a sun sensor automatically drops motorized thermal curtains, holding in heat.

When sun returns, sensor raises curtains for direct and indirect gain. Lower floor of addition includes a hot tub (left), water "wall" (just left of door), and living room (right). Deck and new bedrooms with water "walls" are upstairs.

Trombe wall heats a stack of rooms

The jaunty tower shown here contains two bedrooms and a study stacked forthrightly one above another. Since the added rooms are almost fully detached from the main house, they required an independent heating system. An unvented concrete-block Trombe wall was chosen as the solar strategy, primarily because it delivers its heat in the evening, when the bedrooms need it. Since this was to be new construction, the wall could also be used as a structural wall.

The exterior surface of the blocks is covered with selective-surface foil. The flat-black foil enhances solar absorption and greatly retards reradiation of the solar heat, so no night insulation is necessary between the wall and glazing. Round vents purchased at a marine supply store vent the space in summer and lend a decorative touch. A retractable awning has since been added to shade the glazing in summer.

Through its first Pennsylvania winter, the addition posed no extra heating burden on the house: the owners reported no increase in their utility bills.

Addition architect: Don Prowler/South Street Design.

Inside, Trombe wall (rear) is indistinguishable from conventional frame wall at right. Baseboard unit provides back-up heat when needed.

Outside, Trombe wall glazing resembles large windows; small bedroom window (shown in photo above) can be seen through glazing.

All wrapped up for winter

Built along a north-south axis, with bedrooms to the south, this Pennsylvania house was an unlikely candidate for solar heating. But now a solar addition, extending westward to form a new south wall for solar gain, wraps the north wall in a blanket of warmth.

Essentially a single room, the addition begins on the west as a foyer-entertainment area, and ends on the east as a living room. The flooring changes from tile in the direct gain foyer to cozy carpet in the living room. Air warmed in the direct gain space and by a heat-circulating fireplace is ducted from a new balcony landing to the original house.

Addition design: Rudy Hilt and Mic Curd/Shelter Design Group.

Lofty interior uses maximum glazing to make the most of limited southern exposure. Thermal shades seal in heat on winter nights, seal it out on summer days.

Cedar-clad addition wraps around north side of brick house, adding space, solar energy, and insulation.

Opposite view from photo above shows how new entry becomes new living room. Old north wall is at right.

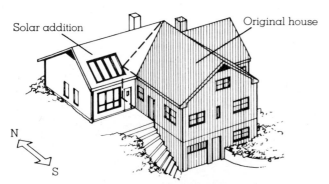

Solar addition

Original house

N

S

Old and new fit together harmoniously. Addition solves problem of poor solar orientation.

Holding on to hard-earned gains

The owners of this house in Seattle were amply repaid when they remodeled for energy conservation as well as solar heating; a thorough weatherization job set the stage for the solar system. Now, though the house has a new second floor, breakfast room, and sunspace, it costs less to heat than before.

The sunspace generates a convective loop that — with the help of a small fan — circulates warm air throughout the house. Because of its large glazed area and low mass, the space would tend to overheat in a very sunny region, but it's appropriate in the Pacific Northwest. Automatic power venting prevents over-heating both on unusually bright winter days and in summer (when the overhead glazing is also shaded).

The new direct gain breakfast room also contrib-utes heat to the rest of the house. As a bonus, the designer included a deck above it with access from the new master bedroom.

Remodeling design: Tim Magee/Rainshadow.

Two-story sunspace with balcony is heart of addition. To its right is new direct gain breakfast room with deck above.

Plain-Jane south wall ignored its solar potential. House was ripe for solar remodeling.

Low-mass, high-glass space works well under cloudy skies in the Northwest, where tempera-tures are usually mild. Greenhouse cloth (see top photo) shades overhead glazing in summer. Stairs connect breakfast room and sunspace.

FARMHOUSE TRANSFORMED

An old farmhouse set idyllically in the Pennsylvania countryside served as the starting point for this extensive solar remodeling project. An 1800-square-foot addition more than doubled the house's size — and more than doubled its efficiency. In its first winter, the transformed home used only the sun and two cords of firewood to warm a family of seven.

The site slopes gently southward from a wooded ridge to the north, providing excellent wintertime solar exposure and shelter from northerly winds. The addition follows the ridge eastward, and the finished home has nearly ideal solar siting, orientation, and protective landscaping.

Added rooms include a new kitchen-dining area, a family room, and upstairs bedrooms. All are heated by a large sunspace that also extends across the southern face of the original farmhouse, which remains essentially unchanged within the enveloping glass. The old stone foundation serves as thermal storage mass for the sunspace and also functions as a Trombe wall.

The double-glazed sunspace collects warm air and delivers it to the house by convection to upper rooms and to the attic. From the attic, a continuous air space runs between double north walls to the basement and crawlspace. Spaces between the floorboards allow air to move from this area back to the sunspace. Together,

the airtight north walls and the airspace between them provide more than R-40 insulation. (This type of construction is called "envelope" or "double-shell" construction.)

In summer, a 3-foot-diameter earth tube delivers cool air to the crawlspace and house. The sunspace acts as a thermal chimney (see page 22), drawing warm air into the attic, where it's exhausted through cupola vents.

Addition design: Alan Amenta/Conestoga Construction Co.

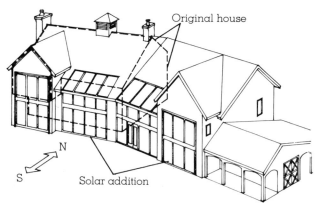

Drawing shows how addition extends original house eastward, adding southern exposure.

Remodeled country home, more than doubled in size, looks out on trees and fields – and a happy solar future. New forms echo the old.

Turn-of-the-century farmhouse is the nucleus. Original clapboard and fieldstone exterior walls now add drama to new interior.

Enveloping sunspace serves as an entry airlock, indoor-outdoor living space, and solar heater. Kitchen-dining area and family room open into it.

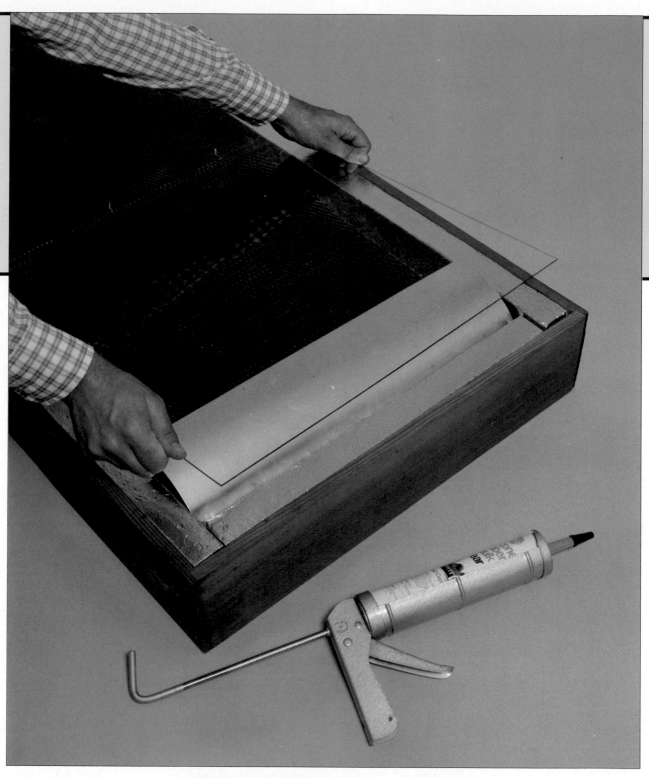

Window box solar heater takes shape as glazing is added. Visible are its black metal-lath absorber, foil-faced foam insulation, and curved baffle. Clear silicone will seal glass. Construction details begin on page 84.

PROJECT IDEAS

BATCH WATER HEATER

A batch water heater is one of the most cost-effective solar projects you can build. It can pay for itself, typically, in 2 to 5 years, and often in less time, depending on tax credits and local costs of materials. The heater shown in the drawing at right can be built from readily available materials in a few weekends. However, it's a project only for the experienced do-it-yourselfer and requires knowledge of home plumbing. It may also require a building permit; consult your local building department before starting.

How it works

Like a full hose lying in a sunny garden, a batch water heater just sits in the sun and gets hot. In most climates the heater shown will easily heat 30 gallons of water to 110°F/43°C or higher by midafternoon on a sunny summer day.

Designed to function as a preheater for your conventional water heater, the batch heater is connected to your cold-water line in such a way that water will pass through it before moving on to the conventional heater. The batch heater must be located near the conventional heater to avoid excessive heat-loss over long plumbing runs, and must face within 30 degrees of solar south (see pages 26–27) in an unshaded location; it must also be tilted up at an angle from the horizontal that matches your latitude.

The heater can function all year in nonfreezing climates, but must be drained during the winter in colder regions. If the heater will be used most of the year, two layers of inner film glazing should be used in addition to a sheet of tempered glass. But if the batch heater is to be used only from spring until fall, and if your

summer nights are warm, single glazing will probably suffice. You'll get most benefit from the heater if you concentrate your hot-water use in the afternoon and evening; but if you simply must have that morning shower, inner glazing will help keep heat in the batch heater at night, giving you some benefit from it in the morning.

The design at right has two other performance-enhancing features, besides the optional inner glazing: selective-surface foil on the tank, and an aluminum reflector. The foil, available from solar equipment suppliers, absorbs solar energy as readily as flat black paint, but its special coating greatly reduces reradiation, thus keeping the tank temperature higher. The modified involute curve of the aluminum reflector concentrates the sun's rays on the tank for increased heat gain.

CONSTRUCTION

The following discussion is intended as a guide for the experienced do-it-yourselfer. It outlines a suggested sequence of assembly, from box construction, through tank preparation and mounting, to plumbing and glazing.

Box and reflector. The box is built of ¾-inch exterior-grade plywood and sized to accept a 46 by 76-inch sheet of tempered glass on top. All joints are reinforced inside by 2 by 3s; 1 by 2s and 1 by 3s reinforce the outside corners and protect exposed plywood edges. Resorcinol glue and woodscrews assure a rigid assembly.

A pattern for the involute curves of the reflector is included here (see detail **B**); you can scale

it up to full size and use it as a guide for cutting out the plywood ribs that support the reflector and strengthen the box; the ribs are screwed to 2 by 3 crosspieces.

After assembling the box, you should make the frame for the optional inner glazing and cut the 1 by 2s for the glazing bars that will hold down the outer, tempered-glass glazing. The inner frame and all inner surfaces of the box should be finished with several coats of clear polyurethane.

When the polyurethane is dry, 3½-inch fiberglass batt insulation is stapled to the interior of the box's bottom and sides, joist hangers are bolted to the box ends, and the lower halves of the pieces of foil-faced polyurethane foam insulation for the box ends are glued in place (note in detail **A** how the halves are divided).

The reflector halves are made of sheet aluminum, shaped to fit the curve of the plywood ribs by gentle bending over a piece of pipe or a workbench edge. Once the curves are about right, the reflector halves can be nailed to the ribs, which will give them their final form. With the reflector in place, the 2 by 4 tank supports can be installed in the joist hangers with screws, and the remaining halves of the box-end insulation can be glued on.

At this point, you should temporarily lay the tank on its supports and mark and drill holes for the tank drain and cold and hot-water lines. Be sure to allow clearance between the tank and the top end of the box for plumbing connections; when this clearance is established, you can mark the locations of the angle brackets that will help support the tank, and screw the brackets in place.

Now the entire box exterior should be caulked, then primed and painted with your choice of exterior finish. Once this is dry,

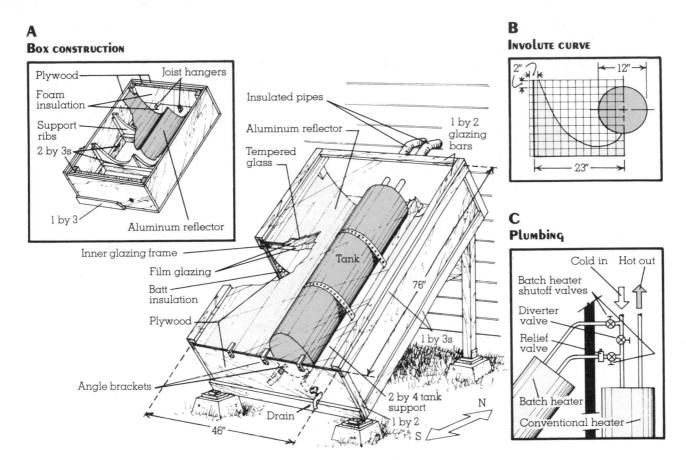

A
BOX CONSTRUCTION

Plywood
Foam insulation
Support ribs
2 by 3s
1 by 3
Joist hangers
Aluminum reflector

Insulated pipes
Aluminum reflector
Tempered glass
Inner glazing frame
Film glazing
Batt insulation
Plywood
Angle brackets
Drain
Tank
76"
1 by 3s
2 by 4 tank support
1 by 2
46"
N
S

B
INVOLUTE CURVE

2"
12"
23"

C
PLUMBING

Cold in   Hot out
Batch heater shutoff valves
Diverter valve
Relief valve
Batch heater
Conventional heater

the box can be mounted in its final location—see the drawing for one suggestion on mounting. The mounted box should be covered with clear polyethylene and left to bake in the sun for several days; this will ensure that no residual solvents are left within, where they might later evaporate and coat the glazing.

Tank. This design uses a readily available 30-gallon glass-lined steel tank measuring 12 by 60 inches (available from a solar equipment supplier or a plumbing supply house). You may also need to install a magnesium sacrificial anode to protect the tank from galvanic reactions. Your tank supplier can advise you on this and provide you with an anode that fits your tank.

Paint both ends of the tank flat black; then apply the selective-surface foil to the rest of the tank. Be sure to follow manufacturers' instructions carefully in preparing the tank for both paint and foil.

When these steps are complete, the tank is ready to be

mounted on the 2 by 4 tank supports in the box. The angle brackets screwed to the 2 by 4s keep the tank from sliding downward; two straps made of heavy-duty plumber's tape are passed around the tank and supports and secured with screws to the 2 by 4s.

Plumbing. Detail **C** gives a schematic view of the necessary plumbing connections. If you're experienced in home plumbing, these won't be difficult to make; if not, this is the time to call in a professional plumber.

Once the batch heater is connected, it should be pressure-tested overnight and inspected for leaks; should any develop, you'll need to shut off the water to the batch heater and fix the leaky connections. After testing, insulate the water lines running between the batch heater and your conventional water heater with exterior pipe insulation.

Glazing. The frame for the optional inner glazing is covered on each side with plastic film glazing (trade names include "Teflon"

and "Tedlar"). Simply wrap the film around the frame on both sides and secure with staples. The inner glazing rests on small angle brackets screwed to the box sides and ends; once the frame is in place, a bead of silicone caulking compound should be run between it and the box sides to ensure airtightness.

The outer glazing consists of a single 46 by 76-inch sheet of tempered glass, widely sold as replacement glazing for sliding glass doors. It rests on ¼-inch neoprene glazing tape glued to the box edges, with another layer of neoprene glazing tape on top of the glass edges to cushion them against the clamping pressure of the 1 by 2 glazing bars. Angle brackets anchor the bottom edge of the glass (this allows rain to run off). The 1 by 2s and angle brackets should be installed with screws to permit removal of the glazing—you'll want to have access to the tank and plumbing. The sacrificial anode, for example, should be inspected every 2 years and replaced as necessary.

Window-mounted convective heaters, usually called "window box collectors," are among the most cost-effective solar heaters and require only basic carpentry skills to build. Installed in south-facing double-hung windows, they collect the sunlight striking the area below the windows and deliver it indoors as heat. They're capable of handling up to about 30 percent of a room's heating needs.

The window box solar heater works on the principle of the convective loop: air heated as it passes through the absorber in the box's upper channel rises into the room, drawing cooler room air in and down through the lower channel and around the central divider, so that it in turn is heated (see detail **A**). So long as the sun shines, the flow of air continues. The operating heater produces warm, not hot, air. Heat delivery is subtle and steady, not dramatic and intermittent as it is with most conventional forced-air heaters.

At night the collector fills with cold air. This prevents reverse convection of warm indoor air through the unit; thus the collector is self-damping and requires no lids or shutters.

The collector shown opposite and in the photo on page 80 is the product of extensive research and development. It outperforms simpler models because it's designed for maximum airflow, and it employs an advanced absorber and superior insulation. Together, these factors make for greater efficiency—as much as 35 percent more heat delivery than you'll get from simpler collectors with flat absorbers.

The ratio of the channel sizes to the box length and the use of curved baffles greatly enhance airflow. The lath absorber presents a large heated area to the moving air, increasing heat transfer. Effective insulation holds in the heat gained and assures a greater temperature differential between the channels; it is this differential, not the absolute temperature of either channel, that powers the air movement.

Design

In planning a window box collector for your home, you must decide on orientation and inclination, dimensions and proportions, and the type of absorber you'll use.

Orientation and inclination.
Though the window in which a collector is mounted should face due south, variations of up to 30 degrees will have little effect on a collector's efficiency. However, the inclination, or tilt, of the box will affect performance significantly. Ideally, a box should be tilted above the horizontal the same number of degrees as your latitude plus 10 to 15 degrees. Thus in most parts of the United States, collectors should be tilted between 40 and 55 degrees.

Dimensions and proportions.
Because of the variations in window sizes, only general directions can be given here. Try to stay within the guidelines below.

A straight collector box, as shown in the large drawing, allows nearly unobstructed airflow; detail **B** shows a slightly more restrictive box profile that's less intrusive in the room. Whatever its profile, the collector must be at least 5 feet long. Of course, inclination and length are related; to install a box of the minimum length, it may be necessary to sacrifice ideal inclination, especially when you're working with a low first-floor window.

Once you've determined the length, design the rest of the collector so that the depth of the lower channel is about $1/20$ of the box's overall length, measured inside (for example, an 80-inch-long collector should have a lower channel 4 inches deep).

If you're using a lath absorber (see below), make the upper channel the same depth as the lower one; with corrugated absorbers, the depth of the upper channel can be reduced to $1/50$ of the collector's length. Don't forget to allow for the thickness of the insulation.

The overall width of the collector should equal the width of the window opening minus about $1/4$ inch for installation clearance (you'll caulk or weatherstrip the gaps later).

Intake and exhaust openings must be at least as large as the corresponding channels in cross section: don't create a bottleneck. The distance between the lower end of the divider and the inside end of the box ought to be equal to the depth of the lower channel.

Curved sheet-metal baffles should be used as shown in the illustrations. The baffles reduce turbulence that can interfere with the gentle convective flow that you want from your heater.

Absorbers.
The absorber must do two things efficiently: soak up the sun's heat and transfer as much of it as possible to the moving air. A flat black, heat-conducting material is needed for the first task, and a large surface area for the second.

The most efficient absorber uses metal lath painted flat black; this type considerably outperforms flat absorbers. Used in plaster work, metal lath is widely available at low cost.

Five or six layers of lath are wired together and fixed at an angle through the upper air

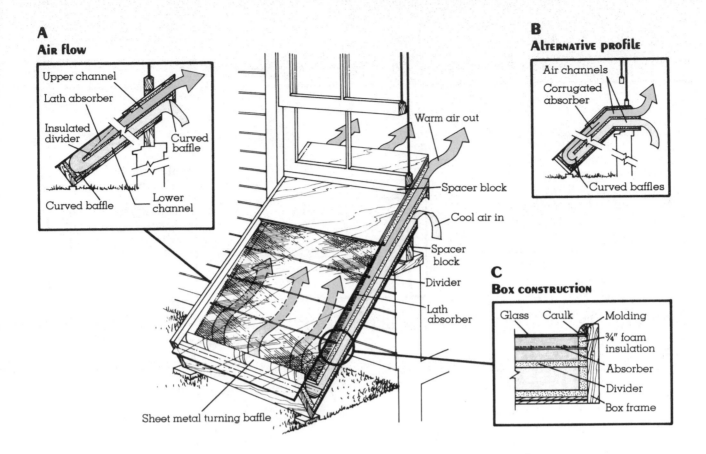

A Air flow

Upper channel
Lath absorber
Insulated divider
Curved baffle
Curved baffle
Lower channel

Warm air out
Spacer block
Cool air in
Spacer block
Divider
Lath absorber

Sheet metal turning baffle

B Alternative profile

Air channels
Corrugated absorber
Curved baffles

C Box construction

Glass   Caulk   Molding
¾" foam insulation
Absorber
Divider
Box frame

channel (see detail **A**). The lath "sandwich" provides a large contact area for heat transfer, and the angled installation ensures that heated air travels through the absorber and stays away from the cooler glass above. Dowels or metal rods inserted in the insulation support the absorber.

Because some sunlight will penetrate the lath, you should cover the upper surface of the divider with sheet metal or tempered hardboard painted flat black.

Alternatively, you can make an absorber of corrugated aluminum roofing (see detail drawing **B**). Corrugated absorbers are a little easier to build, but they don't work as efficiently.

Construction

Build the box of kiln-dried lumber; it will have to withstand a lot of weathering. It must also be airtight, so careful assembly and lots of caulking are essential.

Insulate all inner box surfaces. One to 1½-inch-thick rigid foam insulation with an R-value (see glossary, page 93) of 8 or higher is best; don't use polystyrene, as it may overheat and melt. Make the center divider out of ½-inch foam insulation or ductboard.

Note the construction details in detail **C** above as you build your heater. Rabbet joints—well glued, nailed, and caulked—are best. Prime and paint all wood, inside and out.

The glazing rests on foam weatherstripping and is held in place by stops made of quarter-round moldings, battens, or aluminum angle stock, well sealed with silicone. Screw the stops in place to permit removal of the glazing for seasonal cleaning. The lower edge of the insulated top should overlap the glass by at least ½ inch; this joint should also be sealed with silicone. (Tip: Before glazing, cover the completed box with clear polyethylene and let it bake in the sun for a few days to evaporate any residual solvents that might later collect underneath the glazing.)

Installation

Support the collector on pier footings or concrete blocks. Measure and cut spacer blocks as shown; glue and nail them to the box. Finally, lower the window sash and weatherstrip and caulk all joints between the collector box and the window and frame. Don't forget the gap between the sashes of the window.

Project design: W. Scott Morris

INTERIOR INSULATING SHUTTERS

For effective insulation at fairly low cost, it's hard to beat foam-based interior shutters. Set in or against your windows at night and on cold days, they'll make a marked difference in your comfort—and your heating bill. As part of an overall solar design, they help to prevent the nighttime escape of solar energy captured during the day. (Caution: Foam insulation is flammable; never use it where a fire hazard exists.)

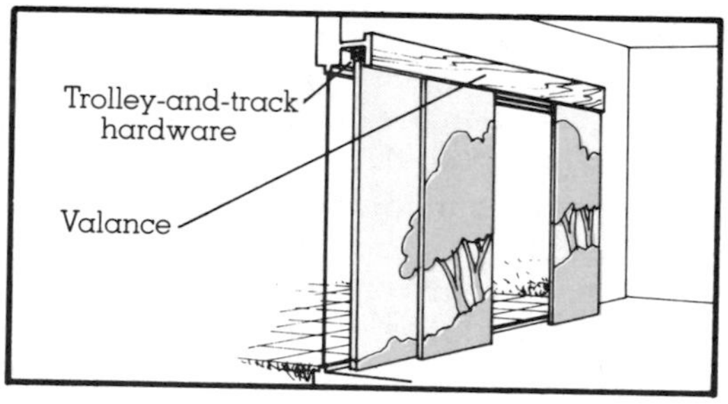

Design

The illustrations at right show a basic insulating panel and four ways it can be used as a shutter. As you can see, it's nothing more than a core of ¾ to 1½-inch-thick foil-faced foam insulation set in a light wood frame (with heat-reflective foil facing the room when the shutters are closed), then faced and edged to harmonize with your decor.

Panels can be fixed or hinged. Fixed panels (see detail **A**) are the least expensive and can be put up and taken down as needed. They're a good choice for north-facing windows that should be shuttered day and night during the heating season.

Hinged or sliding panels are best for shutters requiring daily operation. Use a bifold design (see detail **B**) or sliding shutters (detail **C**) for larger windows or where swing is restricted.

Mounting

Mount fixed panels by using nylon self-gripping fasteners, magnetic strips or catches, or just friction against the inside window casing; no edging or frame is necessary. Hinged shutters require a frame in which to anchor

A
Fixed shutter

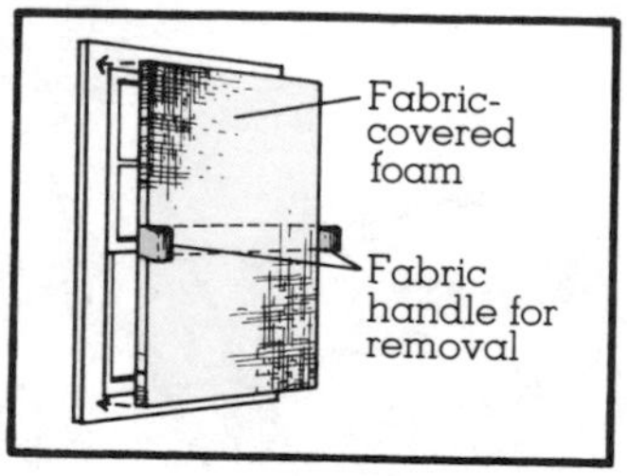

Fabric-covered foam

Fabric handle for removal

B
Bifold shutters

Wood frame

Wood or fabric facing

Foil-faced foam insulation

C
Sliding shutters

Trolley-and-track hardware

Valance

the hinges securely. Sliding shutters make use of commercial trolley-and-track systems.

When you mount your shutters, be sure they fit snugly enough to break the convective air loop between the window glass and the room. Foam weatherstripping between the shutter and window casing is usually the simplest answer for hinged and fixed designs. Use a valance with sliding shutters.

(Note: If your windows are prone to condensation and you can't achieve a really tight seal between shutter and window, it's best to simply use heavy draperies; these will provide some insulation against radiant—but not convective—heat loss.)

Exterior Insulating Shutters

Reflective insulating shutters can do triple duty as insulators, gain enhancers, and shading devices; they're usually inexpensive and easy to build.

When closed, the shutters shown at right are effective insulators against both nighttime heat loss in winter and daytime heat gain in summer; open, their reflective inner surfaces bounce solar energy into the room. On hot days they can be positioned to afford some shade while still allowing you to open the window.

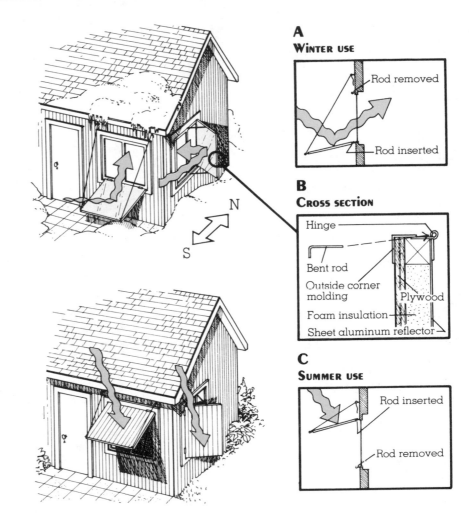

A

WINTER USE

Rod removed

Rod inserted

B

CROSS SECTION

Hinge

Bent rod

Outside corner molding

Plywood

Foam insulation

Sheet aluminum reflector

C

SUMMER USE

Rod inserted

Rod removed

Design

The shutter in this design is simply a framed panel of foam insulation faced with sheet aluminum and backed by exterior plywood for weather resistance. The double-sided hinge design allows the hinges to act as catches as well. For east and west-facing windows, place hinges at both sides; for south-facing windows, place hinges at top and bottom (see drawings).

This is an adaptable design, but bear in mind that it has some limitations. Harsh weather can warp or damage exterior shutters, so use exterior-grade materials, and build them to last. For ease of construction and safety of operation, cover large windows with sectioned shutters rather than single ones. Always use weatherstripping to achieve a tight seal with window frames or casings.

Construction

Size each panel frame to fit on or into the existing window casing. Build the frame of straight, kiln-dried lumber at least 2 by 2 inches, using accurate butt joints, well nailed and glued. Using the frame as a guide, measure and cut the drop-in foam panel, the aluminum reflector, and the plywood backing panel.

Assemble each shutter by first gluing and nailing the plywood to the frame. Prime and paint or varnish all wood inside and out before gluing in the foam and adding the reflector. Use aluminum or prefinished wood corner molding to trim the panel as shown.

Select strong hinges with removable pins. Mount one pair to the top or side of the finished shutter, depending on window orientation (see illustration above). Fasten the shutter in position on the window, then attach the opposite set of hinges.

Replace the hinge pins with pieces of rustproof metal rod (copper, brass, or aluminum—even a rustproof nail), bent as shown in detail **B**. Now your shutter will open from either side, or from top or bottom. The new, easily removed pins allow you to use the hinges as catches when the shutters are closed.

A trip to a hardware store will yield all manner of devices to hold the shutter at various angles. Look for sliding-rod casement operators or trunk lid hardware, for example. You can also use a rope-and-pulley system.

Project design: William Shurcliff

Lightweight Awning

If your home overheats in summer, the best solution is to block the sun before—not after—it enters your windows. Here's a simple design that does just that, without cutting off access to cooling breezes as shutters would. Especially effective on south-facing windows or doors, this lightweight awning provides shade in summer and is easily removed to allow solar gain in winter.

This is an easy one-day project for anyone—or any team—with minimal carpentry skills and the ability to sew a straight seam.

Design

Use ultraviolet-resistant fabric made for awnings or boat covers (look in the Yellow Pages under "Awnings," "Canvas Products," or "Boat Covers, Tops & Upholstery"). Make the lightweight metal frame from thinwall electrical conduit, available at most home supply stores. Size the frame to overlap your south-facing window or door by at least one stud-space on each side; this will enhance the awning's effectiveness before and after noon.

The awning should project far enough from the house to shade the entire door or window from the lowest summertime sun in your area. Work out the design and dimensions of your awning with a scale drawing.

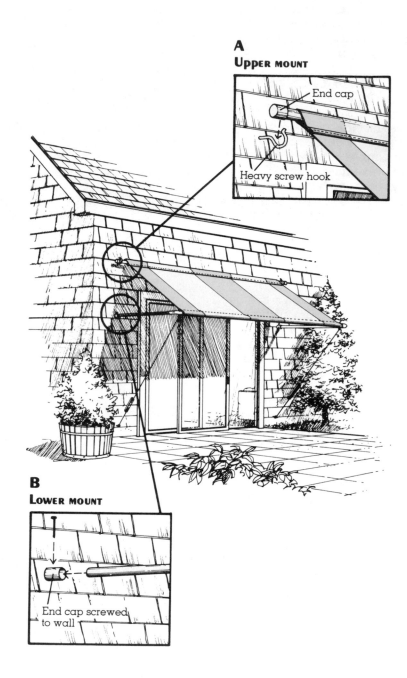

A
UPPER MOUNT
End cap
Heavy screw hook

B
LOWER MOUNT
End cap screwed to wall

Construction

Once you've determined the sizes of the framing members and the fabric, you're ready to begin the simple construction. Cut and seam the fabric and sew sleeves in the ends, as indicated in the illustration. Cut sections of conduit according to your drawing.

When you assemble the frame and fabric, use elbow connectors to make connections between lengths of conduit.

The upper tube rests in two large screw hooks. The two side tubes are supported by conduit end caps screwed to the wall.

Seal all mounting holes with silicone caulking compound.

For security against the wind, fasten the side support tubes to the end caps by slipping nails through drilled holes. For added security, attach the optional guy wires shown.

Insulating/Diffusing Panels for Skylights

A skylight can be a bane or a blessing, depending on the thought that goes into its design and installation. In our enthusiasm for skylights, we often forget their possible drawbacks: daytime glare, overheating in summer, and nighttime heat loss in winter.

An insulating/diffusing panel can be a good solution to these problems; you can mount it permanently, or adapt it for seasonal use, as shown.

Installed, the panel creates a dead-air space between room and skylight, cutting heat loss; it also diffuses direct solar gain. (You get nearly as much gain as you would without the panel, but it's spread more uniformly around the room.)

Make the panel of translucent acrylic or other plastic glazing. You can also use almost any other

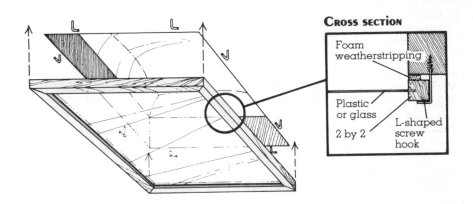

Cross section
Foam weatherstripping
Plastic or glass
2 by 2
L-shaped screw hook

translucent glazing, but most types will reduce solar gain. (Of course, this is sometimes desirable.)

Mount the glazing in a prefinished wooden frame dadoed to receive it. Attach foam or felt

weatherstripping to the frame's upper edge, and mount the assembly by screwing it directly to the ceiling, or by means of the swiveling L-shaped screw hooks shown. These permit easy removal of the panel.

Skylight Shutters

Louvered shutters can be an attractive solution to the problem of glare-producing skylights up to about 3 feet square. Buy your shutters cut to size or trim them yourself. Install L-shaped screw hooks, magnetic catches, and open cabinet pulls as shown.

Mount the shutters just as you would on a window, then attach taut guide wires as shown. When the shutters are closed, the magnetic catches secure them to the ceiling; when the unit is opened, the screw hooks slide along the guide wires and hold the shutters up in a folded position.

Remember that this system is for shading only—not for insulation; use it where nighttime heat loss is not a problem.

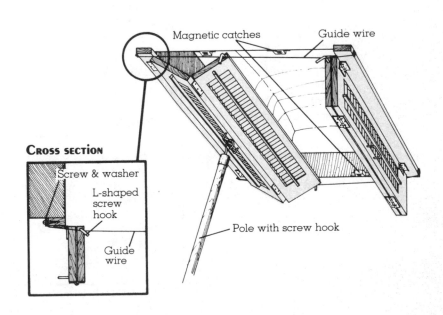

Magnetic catches   Guide wire

Cross section
Screw & washer
L-shaped screw hook
Guide wire
Pole with screw hook

TEMPERING SOLAR GAIN

Think of south-facing windows as solar collectors. In some climates, even single-glazed, unshuttered windows can gain more heat during the day than they lose during the night. Yet sunny windows present a continuing problem: even in winter they tend to create hot spots, sometimes to the point where you're tempted to draw the blinds during the day and sacrifice the free solar heat.

Clear and translucent acrylic glazing, available from plastics dealers in double-wall sheets (see detail **B**), offers a way around this problem. This material admits nearly as much solar energy as regular window glass, but in a diffuse form that eliminates hot spots. It can also serve as insulation when sealed against an inner window frame or casing with weatherstripping.

The fixed and bifold panels shown at right represent two basic approaches to using double-wall acrylic glazing indoors. Both use simple wooden frames sized to match the window casing and dadoed to receive the glazing (see detail **A**).

You can mount the fixed panel permanently or fasten it with L-shaped screw hooks for easy removal. Hang the bifold shutters just as you would hang regular shutters. Both designs should be weatherstripped if they are to function as storm windows; if not, weatherstripping can be omitted.

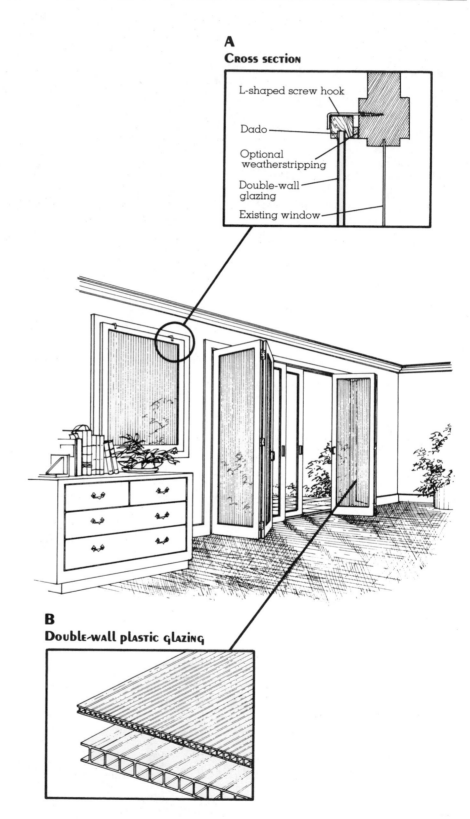

A
CROSS SECTION
- L-shaped screw hook
- Dado
- Optional weatherstripping
- Double-wall glazing
- Existing window

B
Double-wall plastic glazing

Thermal Furniture

Thermal storage mass plays an important role in solar designs—not just because it stores heat for later release, but also because it can absorb excess BTUs and keep sun-warmed spaces from over-heating. Thus, thermal storage mass can make you more comfortable by day as well as by night.

The ubiquitous water-filled drums characteristic of pioneering solar designs have never gained much favor with the decor-conscious; but thermal furniture, like the bench shown at right, can provide water-based thermal storage without creating an eyesore.

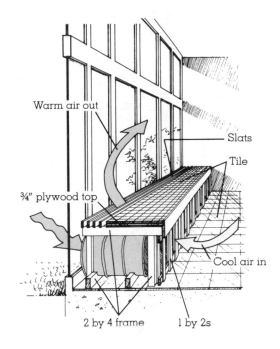

Warm air out
Slats
Tile
¾" plywood top
Cool air in
2 by 4 frame   1 by 2s

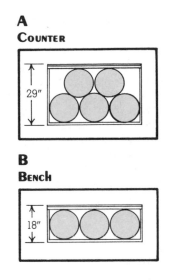

A Counter
29"

B Bench
18"

Using water as thermal mass

Water absorbs about twice as much heat as masonry per unit of volume, making it an efficient storage medium. Water is heavy, though, weighing about 8.34 pounds per gallon. While concrete slab floors will generally support the extra weight, raised wooden floors might not, and reinforcement may well be necessary. Always consult your building department before you begin.

Be sure to buy your containers through a reputable supplier. Used containers can be a real bargain, but you need to be sure their original contents don't pose a health hazard. (In the Yellow Pages, look under "Solar Energy" for advice, "Barrels & Drums" for a source of supply.)

Rustproof your metal containers inside and out with two coats of rustproofing paint. Then, when the containers are in place and filled, add a rounded teaspoon of sodium sulfite (available at chemical supply houses) for each 2 gallons of water. This chemical combines with dissolved oxygen and forms a non-corrosive solution.

With nonmetallic containers, corrosion is not a problem, but algae may be. Whatever kind of containers you use, add a half-teaspoon of copper sulphate per gallon of water to keep algae at bay.

Seal all containers thoroughly with a recommended sealant (consult your supplier). Even after you've taken all necessary precautions, be sure that the design of your thermal furniture allows you access to the containers in case of leaks.

Design

The thermal bench shown above stands against floor-length windows, and consists of a 2 by 4 frame supporting a tile-covered plywood top. A screen made of wooden slats conceals a rack of drums or other containers painted flat black. (Detail **A** shows a thermal counter with room for additional drums.) Openings between the slats, as well as louvers at the rear of the bench top, allow ample air circulation past the drums, promoting convective heating. This convective heating will be enhanced at night if you place the unit a few inches back from the windows and use movable insulation (shutters or shades) between it and the glass.

A simple rack allows the ends of the drums to face the sun, for maximum heat transfer to the water.

Lengths of 1 by 2 nailed on edge to the frame form the louvered back section of the top; ¾-inch plywood makes up the front section. Cover the plywood with dark-colored ceramic tile; the tile adds extra mass.

The bench is fronted by slats (use battens, benderboard, or similar material) nailed alternately to the front and back of the 1 by 2s that run lengthwise at top and bottom.

IMPROVING HEAT DISTRIBUTION

There's a "lake" in your house—a mass of warm air that rises and pools near the ceiling. Reclaiming this heat for the lower altitudes or for another, cooler room makes good sense.

The drawing at right shows two projects designed to tap stratified warm air. The first, a simple vent, acts like a sluiceway in the "dam" formed at doorways and other interior openings, allowing air from overheated rooms to flow to cooler ones. The second, a fan-powered destratifier, acts like a pump, moving warm air down to the floor.

ROOM-TO-ROOM VENTS

Build the vents from any light lumber. Size them to fit between wall studs, as shown, and finish them to harmonize with your decor. See detail **A** for construction details. Attach vents by nailing them to the studs, and trim the openings with prefinished molding or 1 by 2 lumber.

POWERED DESTRATIFIER

If you like to tinker with woodworking and wiring, consider making a destratifier to bring warm air near the ceiling down to floor level. The basic task is to provide a duct reaching to within 6 inches of the ceiling and then attach it to a vented box containing a small, low-power centrifugal blower. The blower pulls warm air down through the duct and pushes it out through the box.

Buy the blower first; the exact design of your destratifier will depend on the blower's specifications. (Look under "Blowers" or "Fans" in the Yellow Pages.) Size the duct to meet the blower's static-pressure limits; your dealer can help.

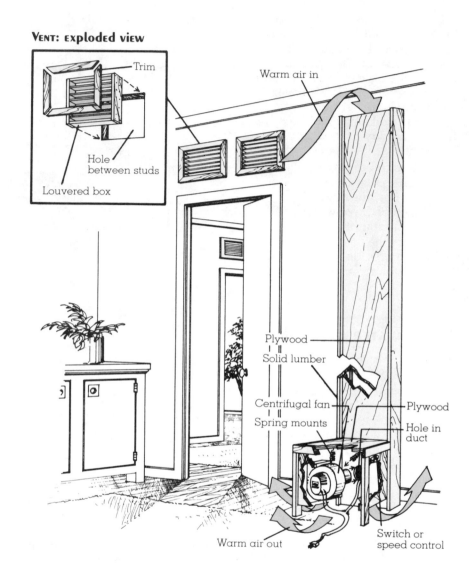

VENT: exploded view

Trim

Hole between studs

Louvered box

Warm air in

Plywood
Solid lumber

Centrifugal fan
Spring mounts

Plywood

Hole in duct

Warm air out

Switch or speed control

Make the box and duct of plywood and lumber, as shown. Be sure the plywood sides stop 2 to 4 inches from the floor, providing a large exhaust opening for the blower. Too small an exhaust opening may restrict the blower and can result in overly rapid air movement, making the destratified air feel cool, even if it's quite warm.

Install the blower using spring mounts to isolate vibration. Seal the blower intake tube to the duct opening with duct tape—*carefully*; you want to be sure all the intake air comes through the duct, not from inside the box.

Wire the blower as you would a lamp or other simple appliance. Your dealer can provide you with the proper switch or speed control. For automatic operation, install a thermostatic switch at the top of the duct; you'll probably want to set it to turn on the blower when the stratified air reaches 80° to 90°F/27° to 32° C.

Glossary

Absorber: A dark surface that absorbs solar radiation and converts it to heat; a component of a solar collector.

Active system: A solar system using mechanical means of heat collection, storage, and distribution.

Air-heating collector: A solar collector, such as a thermosiphoning air panel (TAP) or window box collector, designed to absorb solar energy, convert it to heat, and transfer the heat to air flowing from the house, through the collector, and back to the house.

Berm: A mound of earth either abutting a house wall to help stabilize the temperature inside the house, or positioned to deflect wind from the house.

BTU (British thermal unit): Basic heat measurement, equivalent to the amount of heat needed to raise 1 pound of water 1°F.

Chimney effect: Phenomenon in which heated air rises out of a space through high openings and is replaced by cooler, denser air that flows in through lower-level openings.

Clerestory: Window placed high in a wall near the eaves, or projecting vertically or near-vertically from a roof's surface; used for light, heat gain, and ventilation.

Collection: Act of trapping solar radiation and converting it to heat.

Conduction: Passage of heat energy through a material by molecular excitation.

Convection: Heat transfer in air, water, or other fluid by currents resulting from the medium's falling when cooler and heavier, and rising when warmer and lighter.

Cooling season: Portion of the year (usually June into September) when outdoor heat makes indoor cooling desirable.

Degree-day: Unit representing 1°F deviation of 1 day's mean outside temperature from a fixed standard (65°F for heating, 75°F for cooling); used in estimating a building's heating or cooling requirements.

Diffuse radiation: Solar energy that scatters as it passes through atmospheric molecules, water vapor, dust and other particles, or translucent glazing.

Direct gain system: Passive solar heating system in which sunlight penetrates and warms the house interior directly.

Direct radiation: Radiation that comes directly from the sun, without being reflected or greatly diffused.

Distribution: Act of moving heat energy from point of collection or storage to point of use.

Double glazing: Two layers of glazing material mounted in a single frame and separated by an insulating air space.

Earth tube: Tube buried in the earth, with one or both ends connected to the house; air drawn through the tube to the house is cooled by the enveloping earth. In an *open-loop* tube, one end is open to the outside air. In a *closed-loop* tube, both ends are connected to the house, and house air is continuously circulated through the tube.

Eutectic salts: See Phase-change materials.

Evaporative cooling: Technique by which house air is brought into contact with water to cool indoor air in dry-climate areas; evaporating water cools and humidifies surrounding air.

Glazing: Glass, plastic, or other transparent or translucent material designed to transmit light.

Greenhouse: See Sunspace.

Greenhouse effect: Phenomenon in which heat is trapped in a glazed enclosure, due to glazing's ability to admit short-wave solar radiation while retarding the reradiation of long-wave heat energy.

Heating season: Portion of the year (usually October into May) when outdoor cold makes indoor heating necessary.

Hybrid system: Solar heating system that combines passive techniques with active devices such as fans and blowers to assist in the collection, storage, or distribution of heat.

Indirect gain system: Solar heating system in which sunlight directly warms an absorber located between glazing and living space; heat is then distributed from the absorber to the living space by natural and/or fan-assisted means.

Insolation: Incident solar radiation; total amount of direct, diffuse, and reflected solar radiation striking a given surface.

Insulated glazing: Two or more layers of glazing material mounted in a single frame and separated by insulating air spaces.

Magnetic south: "South" as indicated by a compass; magnetic south's relationship to true south varies with geographic location.

Microclimate: Climate of a very small area, such as a house site, formed by the unique combination of topography, exposure, surrounding buildings, and vegetation of site; may contrast sharply with regional climate.

Movable insulation: Insulation placed over windows when needed to prevent heat loss or gain, and removed for light, view, venting, or solar gain.

Orientation: Alignment of a building along a given axis to face a specific direction, such as along an east-west axis to face south.

Passive system: A solar system using natural means of heat collection, storage, and distribution.

Payback time: Period of time a solar heating or cooling system takes to return its entire initial cost through fuel savings.

Phase-change materials: Substances, such as eutectic salts, that melt readily at low temperatures (as low as 70° to 90°F/21° to 30°C) and, in so doing, store large quantities of heat, which they release when cooling and resolidifying.

Radiation: Movement of energy through space by means of electromagnetic waves.

R-value: Thermal resistance, or capability of a substance to impede the flow of heat; used to describe insulative properties of building materials (the higher the R-value, the more effective the insulation).

Retrofit: The addition of a solar heating or cooling system to an existing home.

Selective surface: Special coating with high solar absorptance and low thermal emittance; used on surface of an absorber element to increase collection efficiency.

Solar chimney: Ventilating device that uses solar energy to create a chimney effect, drawing warm air out of the house and inducing a flow of cool air into the house.

Solar south: True south with reference to Earth's poles and the sun and stars, not to a compass; opposite to the North Star, which lies to the true north of Earth.

Space heating: Heating of a building interior.

Storage mass: Medium that absorbs solar heat and holds it until it is needed to heat the house.

Stratification: Tendency of warm air to rise and collect in layers near ceilings and in upper stories of buildings, and of cooler air to collect near floors and in lower stories.

Sunspace: Solar-heated greenhouse space built onto a house and designed to heat itself (and, in most cases, contribute heat to the house). *Attached* sunspaces can be closed off from the house by means of operable doors or windows. *Integral* sunspaces cannot be thermally isolated from the rest of the house.

Thermal chimney: *See* Chimney effect; Solar chimney.

Thermal storage mass: *See* Storage mass.

Thermal storage wall: Wall made of heavy masonry materials—or an array of containers holding water or phase-change materials—positioned behind glazing and designed to absorb and store solar heat.

Thermosiphoning: Natural circulation of air or liquid in an enclosed space by means of convective currents.

Thermosiphoning air panel (TAP): Air-heating collector attached to the exterior of a south-facing house wall.

Trombe wall: Thermal storage wall consisting of a masonry wall positioned behind glazing; named for Dr. Felix Trombe, one of its developers.

True south: *See* Solar south.

Water "wall": Thermal storage wall consisting of an array of water-filled containers positioned behind glazing.

Weatherize: To use insulation, vapor barriers, caulking, and weatherstripping in order to isolate a building's interior climate as much as possible from its exterior climate.

Window box collector: Small air-heating collector placed in a south-facing window.

FOR MORE INFORMATION . . .

OVERVIEWS

Anderson, Bruce, and Riordan, Michael. *The Solar Home Book.* Andover, MA: Brick House Publishing Co., 1976.

Anderson, Bruce, and Wells, Malcolm. *Passive Solar Energy.* Andover, MA: Brick House Publishing Co., 1981.

Crowther, Richard. *Sun/Earth.* New York: Charles Scribner's Sons, 1978.

Hawkweed Group. *The Hawkweed Passive Solar House Book.* Chicago: Rand McNally & Co., 1980.

Mazria, Edward. *Passive Solar Energy Book.* Emmaus, PA: Rodale Press, 1979.

Sunset Editors. *Homeowner's Guide to Solar Heating & Cooling.* Menlo Park, CA: Lane Publishing Co., 1978.

Wright, David. *Natural Solar Architecture.* New York: Van Nostrand Reinhold Co., 1978.

Wright, David, and Andrejko, Dennis A. *Passive Solar Architecture.* New York: Van Nostrand Reinhold Co., 1982.

SOLAR REMODELING

Alward, Ron, and Shapiro, Andy. *Low-Cost Passive Solar Greenhouses.* New York: Charles Scribner's Sons, 1980.

Carter, Joe, ed. *Solarizing Your Present Home.* Emmaus, PA: Rodale Press, 1981.

Yanda, Bill, and Fisher, Rick. *The Food and Heat Producing Greenhouse.* Santa Fe: John Muir Publications, 1980.

McCullagh, James C., ed. *The Solar Greenhouse Book.* Emmaus, PA: Rodale Press, 1978.

Reif, Daniel K. *Solar Retrofit.* Andover, MA: Brick House Publishing Co., 1981.

Scully, Dan, et al. *The Fuel Savers.* Andover, MA: Brick House Publishing Co., 1978.

Stickler, Darryl. *Passive Solar Retrofit.* New York: Van Nostrand Reinhold Co., 1982.

T.E.A. Foundation. *Easy to Build Solar Batch Heater.* Harrisville, NH: T.E.A. Foundation, 1981.

T.E.A. Foundation. *Easy to Build Solar Thermosiphoning Air Panel.* Harrisville, NH: T.E.A. Foundation, 1981.

Wilson, Alex. *Thermal Storage Wall Design Manual.* Santa Fe: New Mexico Solar Energy Assn., 1979.

Wilson, Tom, ed. *Home Remedies.* Philadelphia: Mid-Atlantic Solar Energy Assn., 1981.

ENERGY CONSERVATION

Argue, Robert, and Marshall, Brian. *The Super-Insulated Retrofit Book.* Scarborough, Ontario: Firefly Books, 1981.

Blandy, Thomas, and Lamoureux, Denis. *All Through The House.* New York: McGraw-Hill, 1980.

Conklin, Groff. *The Weather-Conditioned House.* Updated by S. Blackwell Duncan. New York: Van Nostrand Reinhold Co., 1982.

Langdon, Bill. *Movable Insulation.* Emmaus, PA: Rodale Press, 1980.

Shurcliff, William A. *Thermal Shutters and Shades.* Andover, MA: Brick House Publishing Co., 1980.

Sunset Editors. *Do-It-Yourself Energy-Saving Projects.* Menlo Park, CA: Lane Publishing Co., 1981.

Sunset Editors. *Do-It-Yourself Insulation & Weatherstripping.* Menlo Park, CA: Lane Publishing Co., 1978.

Periodicals

Mechanix Illustrated. P.O. Box 2830, Boulder, CO 80322.

New Shelter. Rodale Press; 33 East Minor Street, Emmaus, PA 18049.

Popular Mechanics. 224 W. 57th Street, New York, NY 10019.

Popular Science. P.O. Box 2871, Boulder, CO 80302.

Solar Age. SolarVision; Church Hill, Harrisville, NH 03450.

Information Centers

American Solar Energy Society (United States Section of the International Solar Energy Society). 1230 Grandview Avenue, Boulder, CO 80302. (Write for a list of regional and local solar energy associations; 29 chapters nationwide.)

Conservation and Renewable Energy Inquiry and Referral Service. P.O. Box 8900, Silver Springs, MD 20907. Toll-free number: (800) 523-2929; in Pennsylvania, call (800) 462-4983.

Solar Energy Industries Association, Inc. 1001 Connecticut Avenue NW, Suite 800, Washington, DC 20036.

Index